Praise

'I have known James Church for a little over a year and during that time we have collaborated on several fundraising projects. His book, *Investable Entrepreneur*, is an excellent guide for every entrepreneur considering raising funds. He sets out a very clear, step-by-step process to creating the perfect pitch document and guides the reader through the key challenges to be addressed and pitfalls to be avoided. If raising equity funding is on your radar, read this book.'

— **David B Horne**, founder and award-winning author of *Add Then Multiply*

'There is a wealth of knowledge out there about how to create and scale startups; however, there is little information available on how best to position your business to ensure it gets the investment it needs to execute on your vision. *Investable Entrepreneur* fills this crucial and much-neglected gap for founders and provides a playbook for them to follow.

If you are somewhere between concept and Series A on your journey and considering or undertaking fundraising, I recommend you stop what you're doing and read this book before you do anything else, to give yourself the best possible chance at success!'

— **Conor Svensson**, founder and chief executive officer (CEO), Web3 Labs

'As a new business owner setting out on my entrepreneurial journey, *Investable Entrepreneur* unveiled the world of funding and investments to me for the first time. It enabled me to not only develop a much-needed knowledge in the types of investment and processes involved, but also provided clarity in terms of where I am as a business owner and where my business is in terms of being investable. I now have a clear vision of where I want my business to go and how I'm going to get there. By following the insights shared in this book, you'll give yourself the very best chance of gaining investment.'

— **John Davies**, CEO, 2DegreesKelvin

'James has written an insightful guide to raising investment for founders of startups who are embarking on their fundraising journey. Being able to successfully and efficiently raise the capital you need is an essential part of the scale-up journey. However, it is often undertaken with a lack of awareness and preparation by the founder and the result is that less than 1% of all fundraises are successful.

Investable Entrepreneur is an invaluable source of guidance and tips that will enable you to develop and execute a plan that gives you the best possible chances of success. It is also an easy and enjoyable read that benefits from the hundreds of interviews and meetings James has had with investors and founders.

— **James McKerracher**, founder and scaleupologist, ScaleUp Focus

'This is a must-read for any business owner trying to make sense of angel investing and venture capital. James has done a great job of demystifying the space with a clear and jargon-free manual. The book is ideal for any startup owner who's new to raising equity investment from outside investors – an activity which is rife with pitfalls and bumps in the road. James' wealth of knowledge and wide network has allowed him to present crucial learnings from experienced investors which will help the reader to avoid common mistakes.'

— **James Merryweather**, investment manager, KM Capital

'This book is well worth reading, providing invaluable knowledge to new entrepreneurs and veterans alike. *Investable Entrepreneur* is filled with significant condensed wisdom from James whose business Robot Mascot has developed a highly successful process for unlocking the potential of founders and enabling them to run successful fundraising campaigns.'

— **Callum Hemsley**, CEO and founder, Eloa

Investable Entrepreneur

**HOW TO CONVINCE INVESTORS
YOUR BUSINESS IS THE ONE TO BACK**

——

JAMES CHURCH

Re think

For Rachael and Henry

Contents

Foreword   1

Introduction   7

PART ONE   The Foundations Of The Perfect Pitch   15

1   The Investable Entrepreneur   17

     The reason entrepreneurs fail   18

     The investable entrepreneur   21

     Asset 1: Pitch materials   23

     Asset 2: Financial projections   26

     Asset 3: Business plan   28

     Summary   31

2   The Fundraising Journey   33

     Your long-term funding journey   34

     The bootstrapping phase   37

The startup phase   38

The scale-up phase   42

The exit   44

Summary   46

3 The Mind of an Investor   47

An investor's perspective   48

Presenting a good deal   50

Providing adequate proof   54

Summary   59

4 Creating a Convincing and Compelling Pitch   61

Beating the odds   62

Understanding the purpose of a pitch   63

The approach for creating a convincing pitch   68

Great ideas don't raise investment, a
great pitch does   70

Summary   72

PART TWO The Six Principles Of The Perfect Pitch   73

5 The Three Phases of the Perfect Pitch   75

Phase 1: Prepare   76

Phase 2: Construct   76

Phase 3: Create   77

Summary   78

6 Principle One: Plan   **79**

The importance of a business plan   80

The Three Cs of the Perfect Plan   82

Summary   87

7 Principle Two: Projections   **89**

The three fundamentals of financial
projections   90

Creating your financial projections   94

Key financial metrics   98

Summary   100

8 Principle Three: Structure   **101**

Why structure is important   102

The biggest structural mistake   104

The five acts of the perfect pitch   107

Summary   110

9 Principle Four: Content   **111**

The two core slide styles   112

Step 1: Deciding the content   117

Step 2: Constructing a communication
hierarchy   118

Step 3: Writing the content   119

Summary   121

10 Principle Five: Clarity   **123**

Clarity is king   124

Ensuring your pitch is clear, concise and
compelling   126

The most common mistakes   132

Summary   135

11 Principle Six: Design   **137**

The power of design   138

Using design to communicate logically and
emotionally   140

Using design to influence investors   144

Summary   146

PART THREE Beyond The Pitch   **147**

12 Preparing for your Investment Campaign   **149**

EIS/SEIS Advance Assurance   150

Legal documentation   152

The approach for a successful campaign   154

Beating the odds   159

Summary   161

13 Approaching the Right Sources of Investment   **163**

Angel investors   164

Crowdfunding   170

Family Offices 172

Venture capital 173

Private equity 176

Brokers and investor relations 176

Summary 177

14 Implementing your Investment Campaign **179**

The fundraising strategy 180

Selecting and targeting the right investors 182

Meeting and approaching investors 183

How to make investors love you 185

Summary 191

15 Making it Happen **193**

Mistakes you must avoid 194

Embodying the investable entrepreneur 198

Case study: The original investable
entrepreneur 201

Summary 206

Summary **207**

What's Next **211**

Take the scorecard 211

Review this book 211

Join the community 212

Discover more about being a successful
entrepreneur   212

Access free resources   213

Book me as a speaker   213

References   **215**

Acknowledgements   **217**

The Author   **221**

Foreword

There's a nasty rumour going around that entrepreneurs are skint. Apparently, to be an entrepreneur you have to eat ramen noodles, sleep under your desk and do everything on your own for 70 hours a week, for years on end.

This is a strange idea, given that successful entrepreneurship is actually about mobilising resources beyond your current control, taking well-considered risks and achieving commercial success. Now more than ever, entrepreneurs can access vast resources for their ventures.

There's never been a better time to be an entrepreneur. There's never been more money, more talent, more access to big markets, more technology to leverage or more problems that need solving.

In the 2010s, we saw a revolution unfold for entrepreneurs. Thanks to smartphones, cloud computing, faster internet and changes to the way we live and work, an idea could become a valuable business faster than at any other time in history. This wasn't a theory; the 2010s saw a stampede of unicorns achieving billion-dollar valuations in a matter of years not decades.

Companies like Instagram, AirBnB, Uber, Snapchat and Spotify had a lot in common – passionate founders, great teams of engineers, disruptive business models and exciting growth plans.

It's impossible to overlook the obvious, though: they all had buckets of funding. The best entrepreneurs make it a priority to access deep pockets so that their dreams can become a reality. Raising money isn't an achievement in itself (just as filling up the petrol tank of a car is not the same as driving somewhere) but without that money, you can't hire those people, develop that technology, run those ads or build that culture.

The problem for many entrepreneurs is getting the funding in the first place. Entrepreneurs speak the language of seizing opportunity whereas investors speak the language of mitigating risk. To the trained eye, it's easy to see entrepreneurs and investors completely at odds with each other. The entrepreneur shares a big vision, the investor looks at how they can protect their downside. The entrepreneur offers hope, the investor wants security. The entrepreneur points to the moon, the investor looks around for the fully developed rocket.

To bridge this gap, the entrepreneur must create a set of documents that investors relate to and engage with. This set of documents must translate the entrepreneur's vision into a language the investor understands. Documents like a business plan, pitch deck and financial projections are referred to as 'funding assets' because, when correctly produced, they are as good as money.

Developing investable fundraising assets is the key to accessing the money you need to achieve your entrepreneurial dreams. When you have the right funding assets in place, it's easy to convince investors your business is the one to back.

I've always found it strange that so many founders fail to produce the right documentation. They pour their heart and soul into their idea but when it comes to pitching it to investors, they show some random slides and some financial projections they made up. Most haven't even documented a business plan that outlines their strategy for achieving their lofty ambitions. Then they wonder why they can't get funding.

When you're looking to raise significant investment for your business, you must invest in high-quality funding assets. By doing so you'll access investment on better terms, you'll find yourself in a better negotiating position and you'll close your investment round quicker.

In 2019 I saw an opportunity to create a unique piece of marketing technology, now known as ScoreApp. Together with my co-founder Steven Oddy, we assembled our funding assets – slide deck, business plan and forecasts – and we went out to pitch for investors. Our documents explained the vision in tangible terms, the strategy for achieving commercial success and a clear path to healthy financial returns.

In a few weeks the funding was raised at a healthy valuation. We had the funds we wanted to make the idea a reality without giving away too much of the business. This funding round wasn't successful because of the idea, it was successful because of the funding assets that clearly explained the idea in the language of investors.

Throughout history every great business, movement or cause has begun with a powerful pitch. Armed with little more than their words, changemakers, leaders and entrepreneurs have launched businesses, gained funding, recruited incredible teams and changed the world.

Conversely, there are many entrepreneurs who've had great ideas and have failed because of a lousy pitch.

When investors believe in your vision; when they can see that you're leading the way in your sector; when they see you've a plan for commercial success; they come rushing at you with the resource you need. Not just capital, but connections, insights and strategic advice. It's your pitch that opens up the meaningful conversations that lead to your success.

In this book James explains how to show investors that you have what it takes to succeed. His methodology 'The Six Principles of the Perfect Pitch' guides you through the process of creating a perfect pitch, backed up by credible financial projections and a convincing business plan.

James has crafted an excellent book that will help you to translate your entrepreneurial vision into something investors can get behind. He draws upon his real-world experience and demystifies the craft of creating funding assets. By implementing James' methodology you'll soon be seen by investors as an *investable entrepreneur*. When this happens, you'll find it easy to raise the capital you need to launch, scale and exit your business.

Daniel Priestley
Co-founder and CEO of Dent Global, and best-selling author of *Key Person of Influence, 24 Assets, Entrepreneur Revolution* and *Oversubscribed*

Introduction

Imagine there was a way to dramatically increase your chances of raising investment. A way to give you a massive, unfair advantage against the competition. It's what the team at Robot Mascot do for our clients every day. Once we've worked their incredible idea through our flagship methodology 'The Six Principles of the Perfect Pitch', they're 30 times more successful at raising investment than the average entrepreneur.[1]

This puts them in the top 3% of founders seeking investment[2] – and it's all because of the secrets contained within this book.

---

1   Robot Mascot, www.robotmascot.co.uk, 2019
2   Robot Mascot, www.robotmascot.co.uk, 2019

There's never been a better time to seek investment for your business – there's more money and more opportunity than ever before. We're living through a golden age of entrepreneurship. But don't be fooled into thinking this means raising investment for your business will be easy. While the amount of investment available may be larger than ever, the number of businesses looking to get a slice of that investment is also growing – and at an even faster rate. Demand for investment is at an all-time high.

With the investment landscape getting more and more competitive, entrepreneurs are finding it harder than ever to successfully raise the funds they need. In my experience, on average, angel investors will invest in just 0.4% of the pitches they receive. Venture capital firms invest in just 1 in every 150 deals.[3] With most founders needing more than one investor to close a round,[4] it's little wonder that less than 1% of businesses raise money through angel investment and venture capital combined.[5] Add to this a trend among investors to put more money into fewer deals, and it becomes clear why so many founders and entrepreneurs struggle to raise the capital they need.

---

3   Khawaja Saud Masud (2018) 'Understanding Startup Valuation', *Medium*, www.medium.com/datadriveninvestor/understanding-startup-valuation-a393f6fadc6f, accessed 7 September 2020

4   Anthony Rose (2020) 'SeedLegals funding round stats', SeedLegals, www.seedlegals.com/resources/seedlegals-funding-round-stats, accessed 7 September 2020

5   Fundable (nd) 'Startup Funding Infographic', www.fundable.com/learn/resources/infographics/startup-funding-infographic, accessed 7 September 2020

The biggest barrier by far is a founder's ability to articulate their idea in a clear and compelling manner. All too often their pitch leaves investors unable to understand the basics of their business, and entrepreneurs waste their time trying to raise money with a pitch that is not fit for purpose. With such fierce competition, clarity is king – and poor communication is killing some of the brightest business ideas.

If you're an entrepreneur looking to raise investment, then you're going to need to understand the secret to a successful campaign. By understanding the fundraising journey, having your critical fundraising assets in place and being able to clearly articulate your brilliant idea, you'll be in a better position to convince investors your business is the one to back.

Those that understand the secret, find fundraising easy. Time and again they can craft the perfect pitch and successfully raise investment. Of entrepreneurs who have raised once, 48% go on to raise a second time;[6] compare this to the overall success rate of less than 1% and it becomes clear that once you know the secret to success your ability to raise investment improves massively.

Investable Entrepreneur will take you through my winning methodology, 'The Six Principles of the Perfect

---

6   CBInsights (2018) 'Venture Capital Funnel Shows Odds Of Becoming A Unicorn Are About 1%', www.cbinsights.com/research/venture-capital-funnel-2, accessed 7 September 2020

Pitch', which sees founders and entrepreneurs become 30 times more likely to raise investment. I'll also cover the core fundraising strategies you'll need to understand if you are to receive the investment you deserve.

As the chief operating officer (COO) and co-founder of Robot Mascot, I run the UK's leading pitch agency. I've helped hundreds of founders and entrepreneurs understand how to create a winning pitch and assisted them to position their investment opportunity so that they can convince investors.

Having come from a branding and marketing background, I've always believed that when great innovation meets inspiring communication incredible things happen. It has the power to change the world, inspire a movement and build brilliant brands. Robot Mascot had started life as a branding agency, but when my business partner, Nick, noticed that many founders had massive problems articulating their ideas to investors, it led us in a new direction.

Many of these founders had incredible ideas – the sort that could genuinely change their industry (or the world) in unparalleled ways – but they were unable to express them in an articulate and inspiring way. This massively hindered their ability to raise investment and we couldn't bear to see these great ideas fail because of poor communication.

This discovery led us on a journey to find a way to give these incredible entrepreneurs the tools they needed to convince investors and give their ideas the capital they needed to flourish. Over the next three years, I conducted intensive research with hundreds of investors and entrepreneurs, creating 'The Six Principles of the Perfect Pitch' in the process.

I'm now extremely lucky to be able to work with some of the brightest and most exciting entrepreneurs in the UK, USA and Asia. Working with such incredible and diverse talent and watching from behind the scenes as the investment they receive turns their ideas into reality is the most wonderful feeling.

This book is designed for new and experienced entrepreneurs who are seeking their first or second serious round of investment. It may be that you have a brand-new idea that needs substantial external investment to reach its potential, or you may have an established business and the time is right to seek considerable investment so that you can rapidly scale up – whatever the case, this book is for you.

Without question, the number one thing investors tell me they look for in a pitch is clarity around the founder's story and a compelling future vision. If they're excited by your idea, they get why you do it and they can understand where you're heading, then you've got a great chance of securing their investment.

An investment pitch isn't just the business plan condensed into 15–20 slides, it's much more than that. It's an opportunity to tell your story, articulate your vision, showcase your idea and explain why your business is going to be a big success. Fundamentally, it's the sales material that's going to unlock the biggest deal you ever made. Because, make no mistake, successfully completing an investment round is most likely going to be the biggest sales pitch you've ever pulled off, only this time you're selling equity in your business with a price tag of hundreds of thousands, if not millions, of pounds.

Investable Entrepreneur has three parts. The first will explore the key concepts you need to understand before embarking on your fundraising journey. It will ensure you fully understand the current investment landscape and introduce you to the world of equity investment, the mind of an investor and the various assets you'll need in place to show an investor that your business is the one to back.

The second part will guide you through the process of creating a credible and investable pitch, delving individually into each of the six principles of the perfect pitch. In doing so, we'll explore each component stage of the methodology (*Plan, Projections, Structure, Content, Clarity* and *Design*), why they're important and how you can excel at each stage to dramatically improve your chances of securing investment by up to 30 times.

Finally, *Investable Entrepreneur* will give you the insights and strategies you'll need to effectively manage and launch your investment campaign. It will discuss the different sources of capital available to you, how you access them and the best ways to promote your investment opportunity to the most relevant investors.

Imagine knowing that your pitch is so powerful you've got a massive, unfair advantage against your rivals; that every time you submit your pitch to an investor you're going to get noticed; that every time you pitch at an event, you'll generate interest; that every time you talk about your business you'll have queues of people wanting to help you succeed. Suddenly you have a confidence you've never felt before, which only goes to improve your mindset and positively change the way you present your business – there's less fear, less anxiety and less comparing yourself to others – making you even more attractive to investors.

It's like being the Team GB track cycling team. You know that all the preparation, all the marginal gains and all the effort prior to the Olympics is going to add up so that you can win medal after medal, with little doubt.

This is what happens to *investable entrepreneurs*. Time and again they outperform their competition.

PART ONE

THE FOUNDATIONS OF THE PERFECT PITCH

Many entrepreneurs' dreams are limited by the cash they have available to build, implement and scale their idea. A perfect pitch will position you as an investable entrepreneur and help you convince investors that your business is the one to back. Their investment will change your business forever. But before you can craft the perfect pitch, you must first put the foundations in place.

1
The Investable Entrepreneur

An alarming number of entrepreneurs fail to raise investment. Many believe this is down to the demand for investment far outstripping the supply of capital; that there are just too many entrepreneurs seeking investment, and not enough investors. This just isn't true. There is more money than ever before, and more opportunity for you to raise the capital you need to achieve success.

By the end of this chapter you'll understand the main reason entrepreneurs fail to raise investment and what it takes to buck the trend and stack the odds in your favour, so that you can successfully access the immense amount of investment capital so many entrepreneurs are failing to attract.

The reason entrepreneurs fail

There's never been a better time to raise investment for your business. There is currently more money than ever to be deployed into business. Even during hard times, such as an economic recession, those who invest in more volatile markets such as stocks and property turn to entrepreneurs as an option to deploy their capital. Currently, if you have a £1bn idea, there's more than enough people out there to fund it. Heck, even with a multi-million-pound idea there's no shortage of opportunity. There's even companies set up with the sole purpose of handing you the money you need. In all of human history, there's never been a better time to seek investment.

Likewise, there are more opportunity, more ideas and more possibilities than ever before. The invention of the internet kicked off what is now commonly referred to as the fourth industrial revolution. We're privileged to be living through such transformational times – a seismic shift in technology, the magnitude of which is yet to be known. Since the beginning of the millennium we've seen a transformation like no other. We've had the dot-com boom, the rises of cloud technology and Big Data, the creation of the Internet of Things, the adoption of smartphones and the total dominance of social media, all of which have empowered entrepreneurship and created opportunities for almost anyone to make it in business. We now find ourselves looking forward to incredible developments in artificial intelligence, virtual reality, blockchain, biotech and robotics – the transformative power of which is almost unfathomable. It's safe to say we're living through a time in which we all have access to opportunities and possibilities like never before.

Why then, with more money available for investment than ever and more opportunity than there's ever been, are less than 1% of businesses successfully funded through sophisticated equity investment? It's surprising to think that, for every 100 entrepreneurs seeking investment, not even one manages to close the deal. As we've established, it's not because capital's not available. Investors are constantly seeking assets in which they can deploy their wealth, and entrepreneurs offer investment vehicles that will deliver sensational returns, but the capital just isn't deployed and entrepreneurs struggle to raise investment. The reason for this is actually quite simple.

Let's imagine two people who look the same, and to an outsider may even sound the same. However, one speaks English and the other French. They talk to one another, but things just do not get done. They should work well together (they've each got something the other needs), but they're just not speaking the same language. *This* is what's going on between entrepreneurs and investors.

Time and again I see entrepreneurs and investors failing to communicate effectively: they're each talking in different terms. For example, investors want to talk about avoiding risk, while entrepreneurs spend most of their time pitching opportunity. Investors want you to focus on building assets, while founders focus on generating income. An investor will want to hear about proof and evidence, while founders excitedly tell them about possibilities. Ultimately, investors want details around implementation, while founders forever talk about their ideas.

These differences mean that talking about opportunity to an investor who is risk-averse daunts them. If an investor wants to hear about the underlying assets, income is irrelevant. If an investor wants to see proof, possibilities sound unachievable. And if an investor wants to talk implementation, the idea isn't so important.

It's as if there's a wall between the investor and the entrepreneur and the message just doesn't get through. This communication barrier is the fundamental reason why 99% of founders fail to raise the investment they need, even though more money is available than ever. Ultimately, investors aren't getting their boxes ticked and they're therefore not investing in entrepreneurs.

The investable entrepreneur

So, if investors are not investing in 99% of entrepreneurs, then who are they investing in? Well, they're all backing an *investable entrepreneur*. Investors could sink their capital into property or the stock market, but many want to deploy it with an entrepreneur; specifically, an entrepreneur that they believe will deliver astronomical returns. Let's consider what an investable entrepreneur looks like to an investor.

If a business isn't established (and by that, I mean does not offer the scale of revenues found in a publicly listed company) the number one thing an investor will put their money behind is an entrepreneur. Not an idea, an entrepreneur. For example, if Elon Musk starts a brand-new venture, it's unlikely he'll even need to tell anyone what the idea is before he has queues of investors wanting to hand over cash. Why? Because they don't care about the idea, they care about the entrepreneur.

Accordingly, to convince investors, you must be able to show that you are also an investable entrepreneur. To do that you first need to understand what an investor is looking for in an entrepreneur. For an investor to want to back you, you must:

1. Be highly resourceful and able to enrol people into your vision

2. Understand the financial risks and not just the potential rewards

3. Know how to deliver commercial success and be able to create a viable business

It's only when these three things come together that an entrepreneur becomes investable. If an entrepreneur offers less than all three things then an investor will not invest. They're not an investable entrepreneur. It's only when three things come together that you're able to successfully raise investment. It's only when you're highly resourceful, when you can understand and quantify the financial risk, and when you have a plan on how to deliver commercial success that you become an investable entrepreneur.

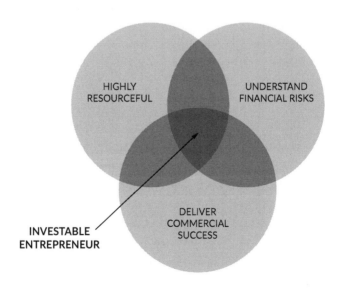

HIGHLY
RESOURCEFUL

UNDERSTAND
FINANCIAL RISKS

INVESTABLE
ENTREPRENEUR

DELIVER
COMMERCIAL
SUCCESS

To show that you're an investable entrepreneur you'll need three assets – your pitch, your financial projections and your business plan. The pitch shows that you're highly resourceful, your projections demonstrate that you understand the financial risks and your plan shows that you can deliver commercial success. Entrepreneurs with all three of these assets in place find it much easier to convince investors that their business is the one to back. They're investable entrepreneurs, and they're in the top 1%. Without these assets, you'll be one of the 99% of entrepreneurs that struggle to prove themselves to be a credible and investable opportunity.

Asset 1: Pitch materials

The first asset you'll need to convince investors and show that you're an investable entrepreneur is your pitch materials. The pitch is the first thing an investor will ask for. It demonstrates that you're resourceful. It showcases your ability to communicate with clarity and to enrol people into your vision.

You'll need to produce a range of pitch materials to run an effective fundraising campaign. Everyone always thinks of the pitch deck. However, you'll need to use three different types of pitch deck during your investment campaign; on top of that you'll need a one-pager and an expression of interest form.

Investor pitch

The investor pitch is a 15- to 20-slide presentation deck, with content that can be consumed and understood without the founder being present to convey the information and add detail. An investor deck is perfect for sending to investors via email, uploading to an investment database or adding to your crowdfunding profile page. It's the mainstay of any investment campaign.

Presentation pitch

This is similar to an investor deck, with much of the content removed, leaving mostly graphics and a few bullet points. Out of context, and without the founder providing additional narrative in a presentation, they're difficult to comprehend. A presentation pitch is perfect for pitch events and boardroom presentations, as they draw the investors' attention to you, while giving you a visual cue and the investor a visual aid to contextualise what you are saying. The visuals will also help an investor more easily recall the information you deliver days, or even months, later.

Teaser pitch

Sometimes referred to as a product deck, this pitch doesn't give away the details of business model; instead it focuses on the solution and the vision of your company. It's often used in initial conversations with investors to generate interest without giving too much detail away. It's particularly useful if contacting investors cold via email or posting publicly on LinkedIn. When done correctly, your teaser pitch will allow you to sell your solution and vision to investors, before then presenting the full business model with your investor pitch.

One-pager

A one-pager is a high-level overview of the investment opportunity you offer condensed onto one page. It covers the key points of the investor pitch and gives investors a quick insight into the key parts of the business model; unlike the teaser pitch. Most investment funds and angel investment groups will request a one-pager as part of their application process, before they ask for the full investor pitch or invite you to a boardroom presentation.

Expression of interest form

This is a vital asset, yet few entrepreneurs use them. An expression of interest form allows you to turn verbal interest into written interest. Psychologically, the act of writing makes for a more solid commitment. Gathering written expressions of interest helps you to build up a number of commitments. Once they total more than you're raising, you're in a position to start closing your investment round. Having more commitments than required allows for investors to drop out during this stage, while not affecting your ability to close. Expression of interest forms come into their own at pitch events, as not everyone in attendance will be able to speak to you directly, yet you can still capture their interest.

Asset 2: Financial projections

Some will refer to the financial projections as part of your business plan. I prefer to talk about these two things as separate assets as each demonstrates a different aspect of being an investable entrepreneur. The projections show that you understand the financial risk involved and the potential rewards available for taking those risks. They'll map out the spending commitments you've made in your business plan for at least the next five years, and plot your projected customer acquisition, revenues and profits over the same period.

As investors study your projections, they'll look for metrics such as cashflow, burn rate, cost per customer acquisition and other indicators of the current and future performance of the business. With the right set of financial projections, you'll be in a strong position to convince an investor that you're a safe pair of hands when it comes to spending their money. You'll be able to show how you've allocated your budget, how you're going to generate revenue, when you'll make a profit and ultimately how you're going to generate a return on their investment.

You've two options when it comes to producing financial projections: do them yourself or get a professional to help you. Doing them yourself is more than possible if you have a head for numbers, and I see many great financial projections created by Robot Mascot clients. However, many more create projections that are wildly unrealistic. The numbers are often far too ambitious to ring true with an experienced investor. Typically, the numbers of customers they hope to attract in the first few months and years is too optimistic, and their marketing budget just doesn't match the level of acquisition they project. Key overheads are often missing, and staff recruitment and turnover are not properly considered.

If opting for a professional approach, do not just approach your current accountant. While they're great at running your everyday accounts (documenting what's happened in the past), they're not always experienced at putting together a set of projections that forecast the future. They may also be more used to producing forecasts for debt finance and lack the necessary experience in producing projections to attract equity investment. You must make sure you use someone who's an expert in this area. Ideally, investment is the main focus of their business, and they don't get involved with day-to-day accounting.

An investor will often want to see these financial assets:

- **Profit and loss projections:** The income and the total operating costs of the business for the period your forecasts cover

- **Cashflow summary:** The amounts of money you expect to move into and out of your business during the period you are forecasting

- **Balance sheet:** Showing the equity in your business by calculating the difference between the total value of your assets and the total value of your liabilities

- **Key metrics:** A set of performance figures and ratios that help investors to quickly analyse current and expected performance

I'll be covering each of these in more detail in Chapter Seven.

Asset 3: Business plan

Investors want to know that you've considered how you're going to reach your goals. It's the business plan that demonstrates your understanding of the commercial viability of your idea as well as the route to achieving commercial success. In essence, your plan should document where your company is now, where it's heading and how it will get there.

Without first considering your business plan, it's near impossible to create credible pitch and projection assets. The plan is your chance to show how you'll create the demand for your product or service, what systems and processes you'll need in place to adequately manage your operations, which markets and territories you'll operate in and when you plan to launch in them.

By producing a business plan, you'll ensure you've considered all the questions you might get asked by an investor so that you can impress under any scrutiny you may receive. Your business plan will also act as a handy reference point during investor meetings and help keep you and your team on track once you've received investment.

You can either create your business plan yourself or get a professional to do it with you. Business plans created by professionals tend to come under less scrutiny than those that have been created by the founder themselves. The information will be more considered and the content more objective. Business plans written by the entrepreneur tend to be over-enthusiastic about the reality of building a business – their timelines will be too short, their plans for scaling too ambitious and their marketing plans or go-to-market strategies lack detail.

If you're thinking of writing your own business plan, make sure you take a considered and objective approach and avoid getting caught up in false expectations. Your business plan will need to contain a minimum of:

- Your objectives, strategy and tactics for the medium term

- Your long-term vision, goals and objectives

- Market research and analysis that builds your business case

- Top-level marketing strategy or go-to-market plan

- Your team, strategic advisors and current investors

- Your investment objectives and exit strategy

As you develop these three critical fundraising assets – pitch, projections and plan – your ability to secure investment will increase. It's important that you give yourself enough time to prepare these assets adequately ahead of seeking investment. In my experience the founders who invest the time and resources to create these assets to a high standard are the ones who beat the odds and get the investment they need. Those who rush through the development of these assets soon regret doing so.

Summary

You should now understand the main reason entrepreneurs fail to raise investment, and realise that by becoming an investable entrepreneur you can break down the communication barrier between you and investors. You also understand the role that the three critical fundraising assets will play in successfully demonstrating that you and your business are an investable opportunity and how they'll help you access the investment capital that many of your peers struggle to attract.

You can assess your current ability to show that you're an investable entrepreneur with Robot Mascot's PitchReady scorecard. Simply log on to www.pitchready.co.uk, answer a series of Yes or No questions, and a bespoke 12-page report will be sent directly to your inbox. This report is designed to give you a powerful analysis of your current situation and will help you identify the areas of this book you should focus on the most. I recommend taking this test before you continue with the rest of this book.

2
The Fundraising Journey

Building your business from nothing into a multi-million-pound empire is incredibly exciting and can be quite the journey. For some this journey will be relatively short – perhaps four or five years. For others, growing their business into a global success story will be the journey of a lifetime. Either way, if your goals are to grow your business into one with a multi-million-pound valuation you're likely to need an injection of capital along the way.

By the end of this chapter you'll understand how best to navigate the different stages of the *fundraising journey*, and how you can do so in a way that ensures you can get to your destination still owning as much of your business as possible. You'll understand how much to raise, and when it's best for you to raise it, as well as the different sources of capital available to you.

Your long-term funding journey

It's often the case that founders focus on the here and now. What's happening in the next 12 months and how they're going to finance those plans is their main priority – so much so, that they forget to consider the long-term fundraising journey they'll need to take to realise their ambition.

Those who don't properly understand their own personal fundraising journey tend to under-estimate the number of times they'll need to raise investment in order to realise their ultimate goal. Because of this, they also tend to part with too much equity too soon (to investors, advisors, agencies or all three). This leaves them with a smaller share of the company on the day of exit than they would have liked, and they fail to realise their financial dreams. It's tempting to try to skip a round of investment and raise more money earlier on. In doing this, you'll exchange more equity than you should as part of the deal. Far too many entrepreneurs build multi-million-pound businesses only to end up walking away with less than £1 million, while the investors walk away with tens-of-millions in their pockets.

By understanding the different stages of the fundraising journey you'll be able to avoid this happening and exit happy that your hard work was well worth the pay-off.

There are four main phases of the fundraising journey: bootstrapping, startup, scale-up and exit. As you progress through these phases, you'll typically encounter up to six rounds of funding; they take place in the startup and scale-up phases. The bootstrapping phase is typically self-funded, while an exit tends to take the form of an initial public offering (IPO), trade sale or management buyout.

THE FUNDRAISING JOURNEY

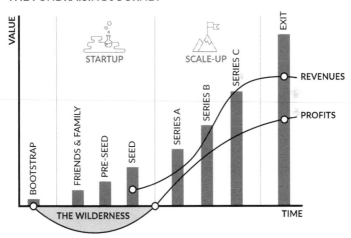

Some entrepreneurs will quickly accelerate through these stages. These are typically tech companies looking for rapid scale, perhaps hoping to become the next billion-dollar business – known as a unicorn. Their focus and enjoyment comes from the excitement and challenge of reaching unicorn status (there are just a handful of these in the UK). Being one of these rare breeds galvanises them to accelerate as quickly as possible through the four phases (the average unicorn takes just seven years to grow from nothing to a valuation over $1bn).

For some, progress through each stage will be slower. While most people think that my company, Robot Mascot, works exclusively with rapidly scaling tech companies, the truth of the matter is that many of the clients we work with are also established businesses. Many of our non-tech clients are more than five years old and have been completely self-funded during that time. They often come to us with a new idea for some tech that will allow them to scale their business more rapidly, or they've decided now is the time to raise investment in order to launch a new product or expand their business into new markets or territories. Either way, the fundraising journey applies equally to all businesses looking to raise investment.

As you work your way through each of these stages, from bootstrapping to exit, your aim is to further establish the company so that its valuation increases. By increasing the valuation you're able to raise larger sums of capital for the same, or even a smaller, share of equity than you sold the time before. Doing so allows you to raise more while retaining more of your equity.

In June 2019, FinTech company Nutmeg raised £3.7m in their seventh round of funding via crowdfunding site Crowdcube in return for just 1.5% equity, whereas a typical business in the earlier stages of its fundraising journey would likely need to part with well over 50% of its equity to raise a similar amount.

As an investable entrepreneur, it's vital that you understand how easily investors are frustrated by founders trying to raise too much capital on too high a valuation. By being familiar with the typical ratios of investment to equity that are acceptable to investors at each stage of the fundraising journey, you'll give yourself a much greater chance of success.

The bootstrapping phase

This is the earliest stage of business development. During the bootstrapping phase you'll test and validate your idea and may also create a basic prototype. You might also opt to find a co-founder at this point: someone who shares your vision but has a complementary skill set. For example, if your idea is a tech product you may need a technical co-founder to help build and test the product. If, like my business partner Nick, you're a creative genius then the chances are you need someone like me, with a more strategic mindset, to deal with the operations.

Many people will tell you that having a co-founder will increase your ability to raise investment. I don't believe this to be true. Looking at the clients I work with there is no correlation between investment success and whether or not a co-founder is involved. In fact, half of my clients who have successfully raised investment are sole founders. It goes to show that if you can show you're an investable entrepreneur, being a co-founding team no longer becomes a talking point.

It's highly unlikely that you'll be able to raise investment during the bootstrapping phase. You'll often fund the business yourself, in any way you can (often with a second job). It's imperative you get through this stage quickly so that you can raise some investment and commit fully to your idea.

The startup phase

The goal of this phase is to get your idea to a point where it feels less like an idea and more like a business. You'll be looking to prove there's a desire for your idea and to identify customers who would be willing to buy your product or service. This is often referred to as *product/market fit*. You're also likely to consider your revenue model and go-to-market strategy in greater detail, create a more advanced prototype than you did while bootstrapping and start building an audience, all with the plan to further validate your idea and get 'market-ready'.

Typically, three rounds of investment happen during this phase of the fundraising journey: a *friends and family* round, followed by a *pre-seed* round, followed by a final *seed* round.

The friends and family round

The friends and family round is the riskiest time to invest. Typically, as the name suggests, the investor has a personal connection with the founder. They may not have a huge amount of money or any industry knowledge, but they are willing to invest a small amount of cash in the early stages of your business to help you prove your concept and carry you over until you can raise a larger amount. A friends and family round typically raises less than £50,000; they get to invest when your business is at its lowest value, giving them a decent share of the business for a relatively small investment (typically between 5% and 10% of the company).

The pre-seed round

A pre-seed round is often completed before a business is generating revenue. Like the friends and family round this is considered a high-risk investment with the purpose being to fund the initial development of the product and get to a position where you're ready to launch to market. This round of investment is typically funded by high-net-worth individuals called angel investors, who between them will typically invest £100,000 to £500,000 in return for up to 15% of the company.

The seed round

The main purpose of a seed round is to fund the development of growth strategies and start transitioning towards the scale-up phase. Less emphasis is placed on product development, and more on developing scalable marketing strategies, recruiting a core team and creating systems that will effectively cope with the demands of scaling a business. Most often, the product or service has been soft-launched and is generating good traction within the market. You'll often need to generate revenue, although this is not always the case – metrics like *active users* are also taken into account. A seed round typically raises from £500,000 to £2m in return for a further 15% equity stake.

	Friends and family	Pre-seed	Seed
Stage of your business	You have an idea	You have initial proof of concept	You have paying customers
Who to approach	Friends and family	Friends and family Angel investors Angel groups Crowdfunding	Angel investors Angel groups Family office Venture capitalists Crowdfunding
Amount raised	Up to £50,000	£100,000– £500,000	£500,000– £2m
Typical valuation	£500,000– £1m	£1–3m	£3–10m
Average equity sold	5%	15%	15%
Risk profile	High	High	Medium
What for	Finance research and tests to prove initial product/ market fit	Create a prototype or minimum viable product to test on real users and further establish product/ market fit	Create market-ready product, develop scalable marketing strategies and get ready for growth

The scale-up phase

During the scale-up phase you'll look to adopt strategies that allow you to grow your business valuation to the multi-million-pound level and position the business for a profitable exit. Typically, this involves four things: growing your customer base; growing your revenue; growing your team; and growing your assets. You might even decide to acquire other businesses to gain access to ready-made resources (such as team, customers or product) that will help your business scale and your valuation rocket.

Facebook, for example, acquired 31 companies before its IPO in May 2012. Some of these acquisitions you'll have heard of, such as Instagram (for a whopping $1bn), but most you probably haven't, such as Spool, which they bought for its mobile engineering team, or DibbyShot, which they purchased to improve their photos functionality back in 2010.

Any number of investment rounds can happen during this phase. They are usually labelled Series A, Series B, Series C and so on, and some companies have reached Series J and beyond.

The Series A round

Typically, by this stage the business has an established user base and consistent revenue figures. The main purpose of the investment is to fund the growth of the customer base and improve the product offering. New revenue streams may be created, or the product launched into new markets and sectors. The idea is to push the business from a customer base of enthusiastic early adopters into a larger, more sustainable market segment – creating a long-term profitable business in the process. Series A rounds typically seek to raise £2–10m.

The Series B round

By this point you'll have a substantial customer base and have proved your business has the ability to achieve success on a large scale. Series B investments will typically support market growth and the expansion of your team to manage the increased demand. Businesses at this stage of the fundraising journey will be recruiting talented teams across business development, sales, marketing, tech and customer support to continue delivering 'best in class' products and services at massive scale. Series B rounds can often support the acquisition of another business. A typical Series B round raises £5–15m.

The Series C round (and beyond)

If you make it as far as a Series C round before you exit, you'll be considered a successful and well-established business. Series C rounds typically fund the development of new products, international expansion and a number of acquisitions. Businesses raise anything from £15m to £100m and the investment is most often used to strategically position the business for a highly valuable exit – the final stage of the fundraising journey. However, some companies will keep going; challenger bank Monzo have completed a Series F round raising $427m, ride-sharing app Lyft had completed a Series I round bringing in $600m and Elon Musk's SpaceX completed a Series J round for $486m.

The exit

Once you've reached the end of your fundraising journey, you'll be looking to exit your business. This is what every investor wants to hear. When raising investment at any stage of the fundraising journey, you must be clear that your intention is to sell the business. This is how your investors realise their return. Equity investments are not like loans with interest, the investors only see a return on their capital when they have the opportunity to cash out their shares. Remember, they're not giving you their money because they enjoy it, they're doing so because they hope you'll provide them a return that will far outpace keeping it in the bank or investing it in the stock market.

	Series A	Series B	Series C
Stage of your business	You've an established user base and consistent revenue	You're a fully operational and profitable business	You're a successful and well-established business
Who to approach	Angel investors	Venture capitalists	Private equity firm
	Angel groups	Family office	Hedge fund
	Venture capitalists	Crowdfunding	Investment bank
	Family office		
	Crowdfunding		
Amount raised	£2–10m	£5–15m	£15–100m
Typical valuation	£10–20m	£30–60m	£100m+
Average equity sold	20%	20%	15%
Risk profile	Medium	Low	Low
What for	Optimise customer base, improve product offering and begin to scale	Expand the customer base rapidly, achieve market dominance and launch new product lines	Expand internation-ally, acquire businesses and position for exit

The chances are, by the time you come to it, you'll be excited for the day you can finally leave the business you've spent the last five to ten years building. As an entrepreneur it's likely you'll much prefer the excitement and challenge of building a business than you will running an established company of 250+ employees, hundreds of thousands of demanding customers and multiple shareholders to keep happy. At the end of the fundraising journey, you'll probably be thankful for the chance to exit, and the opportunity to start something new.

Summary

You should now be in a position to plan your long-term fundraising journey. You understand how the investment terms you enter now will have an impact on the amount of your business you'll own on the day of exit. You understand that you'll retain more ownership of your company if you raise less over a number of rounds, rather than lots in just a few, and you know the position investors expect you to be in ahead of each round of investment. You're also aware that by asking for the correct amount of investment for the stage of your fundraising journey you can increase your chances of securing investment.

3

The Mind of an Investor

To become an investable entrepreneur, you must understand your target audience. In this case I'm not talking about the audience you're selling your product or service to, but who you are selling your shares to. It's often the case that little time is spent by founders understanding investors. This is a massive mistake. To become an investable entrepreneur, you must understand the mind of an investor.

By the end of this chapter you'll understand what it is that investors are looking for in a credible investment opportunity. You'll realise the importance of properly considering your valuation and be aware of the role that achieving market validation will play in convincing an investor your business is the one to back.

An investor's perspective

Firstly, I want to make one thing clear – when pitching for investment you are not 'giving away' equity to an investor. You're selling it. If you think of equity fundraising as a sales transaction where you're exchanging something of value (shares in your company) in return for something else of equal value (capital), then you'll make much better decisions when it comes to deciding on your investment terms.

By seeing investment as a simple transaction between two parties you begin to view investors as you would a customer of your business. Suddenly, it becomes clear why investors might get frustrated when businesses are over-valued and when the amount being asked for far exceeds the current evidence that the business is viable.

Look at it this way: if a house is on the market for 20% more than the price of an identical house just next door, you would want to see what extra value this house would give you for the money, and if you couldn't see that value, you wouldn't pay the extra that was being asked. If you're buying the house as an investment, you'd want to see evidence and sound reasons why this house (which appears identical to the cheaper one next door) is going to increase in value quicker and give you a higher return.

It's exactly the same for investors. Remember, they're seeing ten or more investment opportunities every week and typically invest in less than 1% of them. They spend their days making comparisons between different opportunities. When it comes to assessing your businesses, investors will be making a decision on whether or not your valuation represents a good deal based on these seven factors:

1. You've achieved enough evidence or traction to adequately prove your concept

2. Your product has strong differentiation from other products that already have significant traction

3. You're operating in a large enough market to meet your financial goals

4. You've the potential to command a high market share

5. You've a credible team and board of advisors that can make the business a success

6. Your business plan correlates with the financial resources you've assigned to execute it

7. You've managed to achieve a lot with your existing capital

If these seven factors are not reflected in the deal you're presenting, when compared with the other investment opportunities they see, then you'll instantly be at a disadvantage in negotiations (if you even make it that far). But investors aren't silly – they know when they see a great idea and a business with great potential. If the deal doesn't make commercial sense, they're going to explain to you why they think that. However, before they even begin negotiating a different offer, your initial proposal needs to be within a reasonable tolerance for them to feel it's worth their time. For example, if they need you to reduce your valuation by half in order for the deal to be attractive, they'll most likely not bother.

The fact is, that when faced with a high-risk scenario any investor is going to want a sizable amount of equity; and the earlier you are in the fundraising journey, the more risky you appear. An investor needs to get a good return to be rewarded for that risk. You're not the only business they're considering investing in, and around 90% of their portfolio will fail.[7] With just 10% of the portfolio making a profitable exit, the returns from this handful of companies have to make up for the large number of losses.

Presenting a good deal

Many founders fall into the trap of massively over-inflating their valuation and over-estimating what an investor is willing to pay for shares in their company. When you're at the beginning of the fundraising journey, it can be tempting to give a high valuation to your

---

7 Marianne Hudson (2017) 'In-depth angel investor survey sheds light on angel success', *Forbes*, www.forbes.com/sites/mariannehudson/2017/12/01/in-depth-angel-investor-survey-sheds-light-on-angel-success, accessed 7 September 2020

brilliant idea based on the potential you think it has. By doing this you'll price yourself out of the market and quickly lose credibility with an investor. Once you go down this route it will be hard for you to recover.

The most common mistake I see is founders looking over to the USA and basing their deal on the crazy valuations being given to startups in Silicon Valley. It's so easy to attempt to apply the same valuations here in the UK. Unfortunately, spending any time absorbing information about company valuations in the USA (and in particular Silicon Valley) is going to give you a skewed view of the reality of how investors in the UK operate. Our investors tend to be much more conservative than American investors. They're more risk-averse, and they expect to be rewarded highly for that risk. Essentially, we're just more British about it.

On the other hand, there's the BBC's *Dragons' Den* series. This gives the opposite view of company valuations and how much equity to sell. In most cases the deals in the Den are heavily loaded in the Dragons' favour, with businesses giving away huge sums of equity for little cash. Now, don't get me wrong, having someone like Peter Jones on your team could be a master stroke. But you have to really consider the benefit they bring and the actual time they will spend on your business before you agree to the type of deal portrayed on TV. Many founders are giving away as much as 45% of their company in their first round of investment, and in some cases for as little as £50,000.

This leaves them little room to acquire more funds later in the fundraising journey, and still achieve an exit deal worth having.

It can be tempting to value your company at what you think it will be worth in three to five years, but investors are only interested in investing in you at the price your business could command here and now. There are a number of methods available to determine your current valuation.

1. **Cost approach:** A valuation based on how much has been spent on building the business or how much it would cost to rebuild from scratch. This approach can be really useful for pre-revenue startups and allows founders to value the time spent building the business. However, valuations can be low as this method fails to take into account the value of any intellectual property (IP) or the future performance of the company.

2. **The Berkus method:** This method assigns a monetary value of up to £500,000 to four major elements of risk within the business, as well as providing a value for the potential of the idea. It's great for pre-revenue businesses, but it's subjective. The value a founder assigns to each element of risk will vastly differ from what an experienced investor would assign.

3. **The scorecard method:** This approach is a form of comparison between your company and others

at a similar stage in the same sector. Various risk factors are scored to determine the final valuation. This approach puts emphasis on certain operational factors. For example, businesses with a strong management team and a large market opportunity will normally justify a higher valuation.

4. **EBITDA multiple:** This method multiplies an industry benchmark with your previous year's EBITDA (earnings before interest, tax, depreciation and amortisation) to determine the value of your company. Benchmark multiples can range from 2× to 20× or more. This method is more frequently used towards the end of the fundraising journey and to determine an exit value.

5. **Discounted cashflow (DCF) analysis:** This is the most complex method and requires the most data. In essence, this method looks to calculate the value of your business today, based on projections of how much money your business will make in the future. Because of its complexity this method is often unsuitable for those in the earlier stages of the fundraising journey.

'Valuing early-stage companies is more of an art than a science, especially when it comes to those at the very beginning of their journey.'
   — Cornelius Riethdorf, former senior analyst, SyndicateRoom

By spending the time to calculate your valuation using the most appropriate method, and cross-referencing it against valuations of similar businesses at a similar stage, you'll be in a really strong position to win over investors. Even if they don't completely agree with your valuation, you'll win hearts and minds by being able to explain the process you've gone through to calculate it.

Providing adequate proof

For an investor, seeing that you have proof of concept and market validation is a vital part of their decision making. They're looking for evidence that you can solve a real problem, and that the problem is big enough for customers to pay you to solve it. They're looking for proof that your solution will be adopted by the market and preferred to those of competitors. They want to see that customers will pay a price for your product that will generate profits and that enough buyers exist that you can provide a return on investment.

Before you even think of raising investment you should have some level of proof in all these areas. This is typically referred to as *product/market fit* or *market validation*. Far too many entrepreneurs develop their business with a 'build it and they will come' mentality – wasting time and resources creating a product that the market does not need or values at less than they want to sell it for. If you can't provide adequate validation, then you've little chance of convincing an investor.

THE POWER OF ASSOCIATION

I remember working with one founder whose ability to raise investment changed almost overnight following an endorsement for their FinTech product by a major high-street bank. The bank had committed to hosting the product on its business dashboard for a limited trial – providing the development reached certain milestones. This gave the fuel needed to inject momentum into the campaign and he closed his round soon after. Not only did this show market validation, but also it demonstrated the founder's ability to enrol others into his vision. Convincing a high-street bank to take a risk on a product that was in the earliest stages of development was an incredible achievement.

The best form of validation from an investor's perspective is for you to be generating a decent and growing stream of revenue. This is clearly not possible for all businesses seeking investment. But you can begin proving product/market fit a long time before you're a revenue-generating business. In most cases, this will take the form of a series of product/market fit experiments.

The goal with these experiments is to collect evidence that proves your product is desired by the market and that you can deliver it to that market in a way that makes a profit. This can then be detailed in your business plan and presented to an investor in your pitch. There are four types of product/market fit experiment:

1. **Validate the problem:** During this experiment you attempt to prove that the problem you're trying to solve is important enough to your customers that they'll invest time and money in solving it

2. **Validate the solution:** Here you look to understand whether your proposed solution meets customers' expectations, is an improvement on what already exists and is clearly and meaningfully different

3. **Validate the revenue model:** Your goal in this test is to authenticate your proposed revenue model and confirm that your strategy delivers value to both you and your customers

4. **Validate the market:** Using the evidence gathered in stages 1 to 3 above you aim to define an ideal client and check that they form a sufficient market from which you can make a profit

In the early stages of the fundraising journey it's best to start with low-cost, simple research techniques. I had one client that made a mock-up of their app in Microsoft Word and presented the user flow to focus groups as laminated cards. The feedback was positive, and with this evidence he was confident enough to raise a friends and family round to develop a basic prototype.

When conducting these experiments, you must do so with complete impartiality if you are to get the best results. Don't let your own bias skew your conclusions. If anything, it's best to go into these experiments with the mindset of trying to disprove your idea, rather than prove it. As nuts as that sounds, it will mean that when you do prove there's a need it's genuinely the market (and not your bias) that has defined the problem and approved the solution.

If your research tells you that the problem you're solving isn't important enough, or the solution you're planning on creating isn't one that the market would support, then 'pivot' and take a new direction based on the evidence you've collected. When you've established your new direction, start your product/market fit experiments again so that you can build the evidence you need to convince an investor.

YOUR CUSTOMERS KNOW BEST

One of the first clients for Robot Mascot's Perfect Pitch service was Darren, the founder of a cyber-security startup in the pre-revenue stages of its journey. When discussing with him the problem he was trying to solve and the solution he wanted to create, the idea seemed to have the potential to unseat Cisco, Oracle and IBM as leaders in the UK cyber-security market. However, as we began to unpack the wants and needs of the customer it became clear that they were unlikely to transfer from their incumbent provider to a new piece of unknown tech. As this dawned on him, I could see his enthusiasm drain away. We'd just uncovered a fundamental flaw in his brilliant idea.

Before things got too bleak, I suggested that first he test this assumption (rather than accept it as justified) by conducting customer interviews. If it turned out that they wouldn't be willing to adopt his product, they might suggest ideas that would still allow them to access the benefits. Secondly, I asked whether or not his intended solution could be built as an add-on to existing cyber-security platforms, thereby upgrading them and providing all the benefits of his concept, while at the same time reducing the perceived risk to his ideal client. After thinking for a minute, Darren became excited as he realised this idea could work. All he needed to do was go out and prove this new approach would be desirable – which after a number of interviews and surveys, he did.

By being open to challenge and being willing to take a step back and assess what was *actually* happening, rather than what he *thought* was happening in the market, Darren was able to avoid what could have been a costly mistake.

Imagine spending years of your life and hundreds of thousands of pounds of someone else's money building a product that no one wants, because of your own bias. An evidence-based approach to your business development and your investment case (and the desire to disprove your idea) can save you a whole lot of heartache further down the line.

Summary

You now understand the mind of an investor and what they regard as a credible investment deal. This will help you position yourself as an investable entrepreneur and develop fundraising assets that will convince investors that your business is the one to back. You understand that if your valuation is too high or too low you can scupper your ability to raise investment before you've begun and that you've a number of methods for determining your valuation. Finally, you understand that achieving traction or validation of your idea is crucial to your chances of success in raising funds.

4

Creating a Convincing and Compelling Pitch

When attempting to raise investment, many founders and entrepreneurs will jump straight into creating a pitch deck. They'll run a Google search for slides to include, open up PowerPoint and then stare at a blank screen wondering where to start. When they do begin to slowly add content, the result is often too wordy with a structure that makes for difficult reading. They do their research as they go, change their mind every time they reopen the document and ask countless advisors to review their deck; trying to incorporate all the feedback until they have a jumbled mess of nonsensical jibber-jabber.

By the end of this chapter you'll understand the purpose of the pitch and why it's the pitch, not your idea, that ultimately determines whether or not you'll receive investment. You'll know what it takes to create a credible and investable pitch and how to turn a poor pitch into an investment winner.

Beating the odds

The main goal of an investment pitch is to open doors and create opportunities for you to meet face to face with a potential investor, so that you can go through your business plan, financial projections and investment opportunity in greater detail – and if all goes well, discuss investment terms. The pitch is the key that unlocks further discussion and leads to a deal. Being without a pitch is like standing in front of a vault full of cash without the means to open the door.

But even with a pitch, the chances of getting access to the vault are slim. The average angel investor sees ten pitch decks a week and makes just two investments per year, while venture capitalists (VCs) back just one in every 150 deals they see. It's therefore no surprise to learn just 1% of founders successfully raise investment.

Even when an entrepreneur does have a pitch, it's not like standing in front of the vault with the key in their hand; it's more like standing in front of a vault next to one hundred of their peers. There's just one key, hanging on a hook 100 metres away. Only the entrepreneur in the best shape will make it to the key ahead of the others and gain access to the cash.

Every one of your competitors has a pitch. To succeed you must have a pitch that gives you an unfair advantage and puts you at the front of the pack. Otherwise the odds are heavily stacked against you.

Understanding the purpose of a pitch

On the surface, the pitch is used as a tool to promote an investment opportunity to investors, giving them the necessary information to make a decision on whether or not they wish to make an investment. But by digging a little deeper, we see there are five objectives that a great pitch should achieve:

Objective One: De-risk the investment opportunity

An investor typically operates on the basis of calculating risk. If they can spread their capital across a variety of risk profiles, they're likely to win big. Different businesses have different levels of risk, and with more risk investors seek bigger returns to compensate. A smart investor would look to make a range of investments, some with high risk and high return, others with a low risk and modest returns. The earlier you are in the fundraising journey the higher the risk you present. It's the job of the pitch to de-risk the investment opportunity in the eyes of investors. The more capable, credible and viable you appear against similar opportunities the more likely it is an investor will back you.

> 'Every investment manager has a checklist that they go through. If I can go through a pitch and quickly tick everything off that checklist, then I'll want to meet the founder and talk about the business in more detail.'
> — Ranvir Saggu, ex-managing director – Europe, Fosun International

Objective Two: Show the investment is in safe hands

An investor needs to believe that the money they put into your business is going to be used wisely. There are a few ways you can show this, such as documenting what you've achieved to date; presenting relevant performance metrics; demonstrating you're an experienced team with sector or domain expertise; and presenting clear objectives and validation – all backed up by detailed financial projections and a business plan.

THE VANISHING ACT

I've witnessed the gamble investors take in entrusting founders with their cash first-hand. In one of the first deals I was ever involved with, an early-stage startup, the founder went rogue, just nine months after receiving a £1m investment. Neither I nor the investors had a clue what had happened to him. He seemingly vanished.

It turned out that not only was the founder paying himself a large salary and taking extravagant 'business trips' with his girlfriend, but he was also unable to deliver the tech he'd pitched. In doing so, he'd racked up a monthly burn rate way higher than his plans indicated. Ultimately the business failed, and the founder went into hiding.

Demonstrating to investors that you are willing to put robust reporting procedures in place and keep them informed on your progress towards data-driven targets will signal to would-be backers that you are willing to be held to account and that you understand that they want to be kept abreast of how the company is developing and how their investment is performing.

Objective Three: Excite investors about the vision

Your pitch must be able to enrol investors into your vision. The earlier you are in the fundraising journey the more important this is. Without significant traction or revenue, it's vital to be able to excite an investor about the positive impact of your idea. If they can feel your passion and get excited themselves about what you're attempting to achieve, they're much more likely to take a risk on you rather than an entrepreneur who's simply chasing the money.

'The pitch must align with both my head and my heart. A founder's purpose – why they do what they do – has to be really clear. A lot of founders jump immediately into facts and figures, when I really just want to understand what their business is and how their business is going to change the world.'

— Sacha Waters, equity fundraising manager, Crowdcube

Objective Four: Show exciting returns

You must be able to showcase exciting returns from the investment. At the end of the day this is why investors are investing. The later you are in the fundraising journey the more it becomes about the returns and the less it is about the vision. You need to show great enthusiasm for how big your business could get, while also keeping your presentation realistic. It's no good living in a dream world with unrealistic projections, but equally you should not be overly conservative. Your job as an investable entrepreneur is to find a sweet spot somewhere in the middle: to be ambitious with a healthy dose of realism. Of course, this all needs to be backed up by the market research within your business plan, so that you can provide evidence that your projections can be realistically achieved in the timeframe set out.

'It's very difficult for founders to create the business plan. I absolutely get it. On one hand, investors like myself want you to be realistic, on the other we want you to show us an exciting business opportunity. Balancing those two things is a very difficult task for founders to get right.'
— Jason Warren, investment manager, Mercia

Objective Five: Make it easy for investors to understand your business

Well over 90% of the investors I speak to – whether angel investors, family offices or venture capital funds – say that not being able to understand the business idea is by far their biggest frustration when it comes to receiving a pitch. In my experience there are two main causes for this. The first is that founders are too close to their business to see it the way everyone else does. When you're on the inside looking out it seems blindingly obvious what you do and why you do it. An investor, however, is on the outside looking in; things that make sense to you are meaningless to them because they don't have the context that you have. Second is a phenomenon the team at Robot Mascot call 'omnicular overreach', where founders digress into all sorts of additional future applications their idea might have, thinking this will bolster their chances of raising investment. In reality it only serves to confuse the communication and prove to investors there is a lot more work to be done on the product/market fit.

'In order to get through the door, your businesses must be very succinctly communicated. I need to be able to understand what your business does very quickly; the market it serves needs to be powerful; and there needs to be a coherent message. An investor is seeing a lot of different opportunities and they review each deck quickly. So, the communication needs to be very quick, very clear and very effective.'
— James Merryweather, investment manager, KM Capital

The approach for creating a convincing pitch

The best way to approach your investment pitch is to think of it as you would a sales pitch; it's a tool that gets you into a room with decision makers to discuss the details of your opportunity in greater detail. In the same way a sales pitch tells your customers what to expect from the product or service they're buying, an investment pitch tells investors what they are buying into.

When you think of your investment materials as sales and marketing collateral you begin to realise that you can't please everyone and that some investors are just not your target audience. They may want additional information and evidence (that you don't currently have) or be looking for a dramatically different business model or sector to your own. It's tempting to go away and make fundamental changes to your pitch (or even your business model) based on the response of one investor, thinking this will improve your chances of investment next time you pitch.

Think carefully before you make such changes. If you've followed the principles outlined in this book, then you'll have a pitch in place that will convince investors of the strengths of your business. Don't make the mistake of constantly reinventing your pitch based on feedback from every investor meeting. The chances are they just weren't your target audience. Your time is much better spent finding investors that buy into your vision and can see what you see.

Apple don't please everyone with their iPhone. If they did, all other manufacturers would be put out of business and they'd own a monopoly. There are plenty of passionate critics that will take every opportunity to tell you how overpriced their products are, how their technology lags behind some Android brands and that the battery life is poor. Even so, Apple is one of the world's most recognisable and valuable brands. If they changed their product, their market and their vision because some people don't appreciate the value Apple adds to its market, do you think they'd continue to have the success they've enjoyed for so many years? I doubt it.

Whatever you do while creating your pitch and positioning yourself as an investable entrepreneur be sure to stay true to yourself and your big vision. By all means pivot if you need to, but only when the market tells you to, not because an investor you've just met is sceptical about the likelihood of your success. Don't morph into someone you're not or turn your business into something you're not passionate about for the sake of securing an investor. There are plenty out there. By being an investable entrepreneur, you'll be able to be more selective in choosing investors that align with your vision, rather than aligning your passion with that of an investor.

Great ideas don't raise investment, a great pitch does

It may sound counter-intuitive, but whether or not you raise investment has little to do with your idea, and nearly everything to do with how you communicate it. If you work in a co-working space, have attended an incubator, taken part in an accelerator or been attempting to raise investment for some time, then you've probably come across many business ideas that you were unsure about; and you've probably seen some of those ideas raise investment. You probably think, 'My idea has so much more potential – how come they managed to get investment?'

In all likelihood, it's because they've been able to explain their idea clearly. They've nailed their communication and articulated *what they do, how it works* and *why it should exist* better than most. Their idea may well suck compared to yours, but they're able to attract investment because the investors know what it is that they're being asked to invest in.

Without a good pitch an entrepreneur is just not going to be invited to discuss their investment opportunity in greater detail. Investors haven't got the time to read between the lines and try to figure out for themselves what you do, nor are they interested in making assumptions and guessing. Their time is precious, and the stakes are high. They won't waste their time meeting someone based on guesswork.

Think of it this way: if you're unable to properly articulate what your product or service is to an investor, how are they to expect that you can convince clients to buy it? If you can't inspire them with your vision, how are they to believe you can attract the best employees to work for you or big brands to partner with you? Relying on the power of your idea alone will do you no favours. A great pitch, on the other hand, is the rocket fuel that will get your idea off the ground.

Summary

You should now understand the purpose of the pitch and why it's the pitch, not your idea, that ultimately determines whether or not you'll receive investment. You know what investors are looking for in a compelling pitch and the approach you must take to turn a poor pitch into an investment winner. Over the next few chapters you'll discover 'The Six Principles of the Perfect Pitch'. When you're ready, it's time to delve into each principle, so that you can craft a convincing, compelling and credible pitch that will position you as an investable entrepreneur.

PART TWO

THE SIX PRINCIPLES OF THE PERFECT PITCH

Crafting a perfect pitch will remove the biggest barrier between you and the investment you need to fulfil your entrepreneurial dreams. 'The Six Principles of the Perfect Pitch' gives you a step-by-step method for turning your idea into an investment winner.

5
The Three Phases of the Perfect Pitch

Before we begin Part Two and explore 'The Six Principles of the Perfect Pitch', I first want to explain three phases in which you create a credible and investable pitch. Each of the six principles applies to one of these phases. Each phase is as vital as the other two – to create a pitch that is an investment winner you must complete each phase in the order shown below. You must not start one before completing the previous one and you must not miss out a phase. Those that do, present a poorly conceived pitch and stand little chance of ever convincing investors that their business is the one to back.

THE SIX PRINCIPLES OF THE PERFECT PITCH

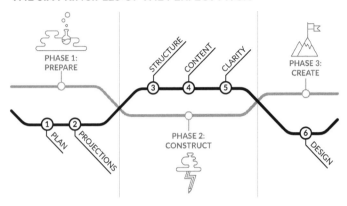

Phase 1: Prepare

During this phase you'll create two critical fundraising assets – a persuasive business plan and a set of credible financial projections. The focus of the Prepare phase is on ensuring that the information in the business plan and financial projections meets with investor expectations, holds up to investor scrutiny and presents a clear product/market fit. This content is then used as a basis for creating your pitch (the third critical fundraising asset) over the second and third phases. It's no surprise that this phase contains the first two principles: *Plan* and *Projections*.

Phase 2: Construct

By the end of this phase you'll have completed the written content for your pitch. You'll have used the raw information from the business plan and financial projections to produce a clear, compelling and logical narrative with concise and articulate content. Your business plan of 30-plus pages and your multiple financial spreadsheets are distilled into 15 to 20 key slides, each containing less than 100 words. Each slide will contain only the most relevant and important information, and each sentence will pack a punch. The language you create will leave the investor in no doubt what your business is and what massive potential you have. This phase contains three of the six principles: *Structure, Content* and *Clarity*.

Phase 3: Create

The Create phase is where the content is transformed into a professional presentation that builds trust and authority with investors. The use of typography, diagrams, imagery and infographics will produce a pitch deck that quickly and clearly explains to investors what makes your idea special and why they should invest. By using information design principles, you can make sure all the content is presented clearly, while allowing the design style you adopt to reinforce your brand positioning, values and ethos. The Create phase contains the last of the six principles: *Design*.

Summary

You now know the three key phases of the perfect pitch: Prepare, Construct and Create. You understand how each phase relates to the broader context of 'The Six Principles of the Perfect Pitch' and you know where each of the six principles fits within each phase. You appreciate that each phase informs the next and realise that in order to produce a compelling and powerful pitch, you must complete each phase in order and not miss out a step in the process. Now that you understand the three key phases, we'll dive into each of the six principles individually.

6
Principle One: Plan

You cannot create a pitch that will convince investors without first having a believable business plan. The business plan lays the building blocks of a great pitch. It's the life-blood of the content and narrative. It's what allows you to consider and showcase exactly how you plan to build your business, deliver commercial value and achieve a return on their investment. To create the perfect pitch, you must first have a believable plan.

By the end of this chapter you'll understand the importance of creating a clear and credible business plan. You'll be familiar with 'The Three Cs of the Perfect Plan' and you'll understand the mistakes founders and entrepreneurs make most often when preparing their business plan ahead of their investment round.

The importance of a business plan

When Robot Mascot started writing and designing pitch decks for founders back in 2016 my expectation was that founders would come to us with a fully formed business plan ready for us to turn into a concise and articulate 15–20 slide pitch deck. However, we soon realised that this was rarely the case. More often than not, founders and entrepreneurs hadn't properly considered their business plan, thinking the pitch deck and business plan would be the same thing. They're not.

It's for this reason we created PitchPrep, an online platform that guides our clients to formalise their thinking around their business plan. Getting the business plan right must happen before you even begin considering your investment pitch, or you're wasting your time. It's why creating a believable business plan is the first principle in 'The Six Principles of the Perfect Pitch'.

Entrepreneurs who decide to treat their pitch as their business plan soon regret it. The content in their pitch is often confused and inappropriate. This is because they've never tried to define all the aspects of their business in one place; instead their plans are in their heads, as notes on their phones or in email exchanges between co-founders. Without trying to pull it all together and write it down you'll fail to consider how each part of the plan links with the others and you'll not properly check and research key aspects of your business model. It's therefore inevitable that without first writing a business plan, you'll struggle to create a convincing pitch. You'll lack content, depth and credibility.

Also, without a business plan you've no further information to give an investor when asked – at least not in a form that has been formalised and polished, and is easily understood. Instead you'll babble, forget important information or try desperately to justify your reasoning – knowing that in reality you have little evidence to support your claims.

Your business plan defines your strategy for delivering commercial success. It identifies the challenges you'll face and how you'll overcome them. You'll consider the risks, as well as the opportunities. Most importantly, it will map out how you're going to deliver returns to your investors.

By putting these plans for growth down on paper, you're creating a physical asset that will support your fundraising effort. It can be sent to investors on their request and be referred to in a meeting when a tricky question is asked. Having your plan documented as a formal fundraising asset only goes to build your credibility – investors will be able to see for themselves that you've considered at length the detail of how you'll achieve success.

Ultimately, your business plan forms the basis of your winning pitch. It's where you can set down all the information about your business in great depth; consider how each part of the plan interacts with the others; and ensure you cover in enough detail all the areas about which an investor could conceivably require information. When you do this, you can be confident that your pitch will hold up to scrutiny.

The Three Cs of the Perfect Plan

Entrepreneurs struggle most in three areas when it comes to creating an investable business plan. At Robot Mascot, we focus a lot of our time on ensuring that our clients' business plans are Correct, Consistent and Credible. We call these 'The Three Cs of the Perfect Plan' and they guide us to ensuring that every business plan we produce is robust, meets investor expectations and holds up to scrutiny.

I often liken an investor considering the merits of a business plan to someone considering buying a classic car. My father-in-law, Mick, is a big fan of classic cars, and I often go with him to car auctions. Standing in a fume-filled warehouse, observing him assess the potential purchase of a 1964 Austin Healey, it dawned on me that purchasing a classic car is just like buying equity: Mick is purchasing an asset (in this case a classic car), hoping that it will go up in value over the next five years. He'll enjoy the ride for a period, then look to sell it for a profit that massively outstrips inflation, then reinvest the proceeds in more assets – such as a rarer car that has the potential to generate even higher returns. The way Mick assesses a deal is remarkably similar to how an investor assesses a business plan.

Be correct: avoid missing content

The first thing Mick will do is check that correct information is provided for him to base a decision on. He'll start a few days before the auction, looking at the online listings. He has a list of criteria he's looking for in a good classic car investment: make, model, year, engine size, mileage and other things. If a listing doesn't have the information he's looking for, that car won't make it onto his shortlist – there's only so much time ahead of the auction to view the cars, so you have to have a list of the ones you're interested in and check those out first. It's the same with your pitch – if you don't include the information the investors are looking for (because it's not been properly considered in your business plan) then it's unlikely you'll make it onto their shortlist.

Most business plans written by entrepreneurs I've worked with have missed vital information. I find entrepreneurs are great at including detail about their product – how it works, the technology they've used, the features it has and generally how incredible, amazing and innovative their idea is. They're also great at documenting their processes and the staff they'll require to develop the product. However, they're less good at thinking about the staff they'll need to operate the core business functions such as human resources (HR), sales, marketing and admin. They also tend to lack sufficient detail in the market analysis, competitor research, product validation and customer acquisition strategy.

Be consistent: avoid mismatching content

When we arrive at the auction, we make a beeline to the cars at the top of Mick's shortlist. The first thing he does is check for consistency: to see whether the car lives up to the listing, the pitch he's seen online. He'll check under the bonnet to see the state of the engine, check under the chassis for water and oil leaks, and (much like an investor checking through your business plan) he's got some neat tricks that he uses to check that everything appears as it should: such as lifting up the carpet in the boot (apparently this is often the first place to rust) or tapping the bodywork for signs of filler (a dink for metal, a donk for filler – in case you're interested). If the car is inconsistent with the pitch, it's quickly crossed off the shortlist.

We often see business plans in which the content, data and research across various sections of the plan do not match up. This can be for a number of reasons; perhaps different parts of the plan have been created by different members of the team in isolation from one another, perhaps they've been created months apart or perhaps it's simply that one part of the plan has been updated and the founder failed to realise that doing this had a knock-on effect on other parts of the plan.

When prepared correctly, each part of the business plan should inform the others. For example, the target market will help define the market opportunity, the market research will impact on the customer acquisition strategy and the operational strategy will determine the HR requirements. The last thing an investor wants to see when assessing an investment opportunity is research, data and information that don't seem to relate to one another. It raises red flags, and means they question your ability to properly run and manage your business. A consistent narrative across your business plan, however, will build your authority and trust in you as an entrepreneur.

Be credible: avoid unrealistic content

The third task before deciding whether or not to invest in the car is determining the credibility of what's been assessed so far. Mick will usually want to see the ownership history, original documentation and an extensive service history that documents the work the car has had done. He'll want a log of which parts are original, which have been replaced and which of those replacements have been original genuine parts. He'll also try to speak to the current owner to find out vital information that might hinder the car achieving its possible future value.

In exactly the same way, an investor will want to see that you have a range of primary and secondary research to back up your claims and that you have reasonable explanations for the assumptions you've made. They too will want to speak with you to determine whether you're able to deliver a return on their investment.

It's typical to see entrepreneurs over-inflate their facts, figures and metrics (whether on purpose or unintentionally). It's all too easy to fall into the trap of writing your business plan from a biased perspective; you may catch yourself being more sympathetic to information that proves your point while ignoring data that contradicts it, or you may try to make your data seem more impressive than it is – all in an attempt to impress an investor. But a seasoned investor can easily see through such attempts and when they do, they'll think either that you're incompetent or that you're trying to pull the wool over their eyes – neither of which will lead to investment. By being realistic, rooting your plan in thorough research and committing yourself to detailed consideration of all aspects of it, you'll be able to ensure you and your business appear credible and hold up to investor scrutiny.

Summary

You now understand that having a business plan is vitally important for creating a clear and credible pitch. Not only that, but you're aware that a well-researched plan gives credibility to your cause and when documented becomes an asset that you can leverage to convince investors. You're also familiar with 'The Three Cs of the Perfect Plan' – and have guidance on how to ensure your business plan is correct, consistent and credible.

To give you a starting point for your business plan and guide you in ensuring you have considered all the information an investor is going to want to know about your business, we've created a free template which can be downloaded from the Robot Mascot website. You can access it here: www.robotmascot. co.uk/free-resources.

7
Principle Two: Projections

The next step in producing the perfect pitch is creating a credible set of financial projections. The aim is to show that you understand the financial risks and rewards by mapping out, in financial terms, the impact your business plan will have on the growth of your business. If the business plan is the life-blood of the content and narrative, it's the financial projections that give ultimate credibility to your cause.

By the end of this chapter you'll understand how to create your forecasts and learn more about the three fundamentals of financial projections: *growth*, *speed* and *exit*. You'll also understand the key metrics investors are looking for to assess your investment opportunity and determine whether or not your business is the one to back.

The three fundamentals of financial projections

Investors are looking to back scalable businesses that come with a large pay-out on the day of exit. Your financial projections are the tool that allow you to show that you can deliver this level of return, while also showing investors that you've properly understood, scrutinised and justified the financial risks involved in delivering on your business plan. Through your projections, investors will be able to see for themselves how your strategic decision making will deliver the financial performance needed for a profitable exit.

At a macro level, investors are looking for three things from your projections: *growth, speed* and *exit*. If you approach your forecast with these three fundamentals in mind, you'll prepare projections that will leave you primed for convincing investors.

Growth

Investors want to see high, sustained growth. Typically, this means showing you have the ability to generate £15–50m in annual revenue. Lower than £15m often will generate too small a return for the risk involved, forecasting revenue higher than £50m per year is likely to seem irrational if you're in the earlier stages of the fundraising journey. To get to these kinds of figures, you'll need ambitious year-on-year growth. The official definition of a 'scale-up' is a business that has 'achieved growth of 20% or more in either employment or turnover year on year for at least three years'.[8] Your projections will almost always need to achieve much higher growth than this if you are to attract the average investor.

Speed

Not only do investors want to see high growth, but they need to see it happening at speed. They're unlikely to want to wait 20 years to get their money back. With this in mind, you must consider your fundraising journey and the speed with which you can progress from one stage to the next when creating your projections. Typically, investors are looking for an exit in five years. You must, therefore, forecast to spend enough in the first couple of years to quickly get to the point of being able to launch to market, and then enough in the next three years to significantly grow revenues to somewhere between £15m and £50m per year.

Exit

Angel investors are looking for a 10× to 30× return on their investment at the time of exit, while VCs want to see the potential for 150× or more. When it comes to calculating an exit valuation, the basic formula is

8   Sherry Coutu (2014) *The Scale-up Report on Economic Growth*, ScaleUp Institute, www.scaleupinstitute.org.uk/wp-content/ uploads/2019/12/scaleup-report_2014.pdf, accessed 7 September 2020

Valuation = Profit × Multiple (sometimes *revenue* is substituted for *profit*). The multiple is a variable figure and will be determined by an industry benchmark (which increases or decreases based on the underlying assets in your business – some of these assets are tangible, such as stock and equipment; others are intangible, such as brand, culture, systems and IP). To ensure your projections are attractive to an investor, you'll need to ensure your profit allows for your business to be valued highly enough at the time it is sold.[9]

Knowing the exit multiple for your type of business and sector is vital. Without it, you're unable to validate your financial projections and ensure that you will be able to exit at a valuation that achieves a suitable return. Doing full valuation research to find an agreeable day-of-exit valuation can be time-consuming (there are agencies dedicated to doing this for you). That said, this post on the Robot Mascot blog (www.robotmascot.co.uk/ebitda-multiples-by-industry/) provides a useful research tool for an off-the-cuff profit multiple for your sector.

If your financial forecasts fail to deliver on growth, speed and exit, then you'll struggle to bring investors on board. If this is the case, you may wish to consider other forms of financing your business, or alternatively you may need to seek help to see if professionals can help you rework your business plan and build more

9   Sherry Coutu (2014)

robust projections that deliver the level of returns required.

PROBLEMATIC PROJECTIONS

Many founders struggle with the financial projections. For most, dealing with spreadsheets is the worst part of the job. But one story in particular springs to mind when I think of the importance of applying growth, speed and exit. I'm not going to use the founder's real name – it wouldn't be fair – but I am going to share their story, so that you don't make the same mistake.

Sally was seeking £500,000 in return for 15% equity – a pre-money valuation of £2.8m. Given her company's current traction and the stage they were at on their fundraising journey, this seemed reasonable. Unfortunately, Sally hadn't considered their financials in terms of *growth, speed* and *exit*.

She'd fallen into the trap of basing her projections on a simple 30% year-on-year growth. Given that she expected to launch with around 2,000 clients from day one by converting some of their existing community, 30% annual growth meant that by the end of year five she would have just over 9,500 users. Her revenue per user was just £5 per month – giving her business just £570,000 in annual recurring revenue. The *Valuation = Revenue × Multiple* formula generated a £2.6m valuation on the day of exit. The maths simply didn't add up. Based on their projections the business valuation would have reduced by £200,000 over the first five years.

By working together with the founder, the team at Robot Mascot were able to carry out market research that allowed for higher assumed revenues, a more realistic growth rate and more accurate market penetration. At the same time, we improved the revenue model and increased the lifetime value of her customers by showing that new revenue streams could be added in years three and four. This resulted in five-year projections that hit the £15m mark with an exit valuation of £70.5m – a 20× return for investors.

Creating your financial projections

Creating financial projections isn't accounting. Accounting is being able to look backwards in time and document what *actually* happened in the business so you can issue dividends and pay your tax liabilities. Forecasting on the other hand is about looking into the future and making educated guesses.

To make these guesses as credible as possible they must be well researched so that the assumptions you base on them appear realistic. For the most part these assumptions will be taken from your business plan. You may find that you need to adjust some of the assumptions as you work them into your projections. If so, it's vital that you go back and update your business plan accordingly. All too often I see financial projections that appear separate from the business plan – they're telling different stories about the same business. When this is translated into your pitch, you'll end up with an inconsistent and unfathomable business case.

It's desirable to include five years of forecasts in your projections as this relates to a typical investor's expectations of an ideal exit timeframe. Remember, your projections consist of four assets – your profit and loss forecast, cashflow summary, balance sheet and key financial metrics. Let's look at each in turn.

Profit and loss forecast

Your profit and loss (P&L) forecast will document the income and expenses you project over the forecasted period. You need to consider three components of this:

- **Revenue:** This is the income generated by the business by selling its product or services. You'll need to consider your different revenue streams as well as how your sales will grow each month according to your marketing strategy. If you're adopting a recurring revenue model, don't forget to consider your monthly churn rate (this is defined in 'Key financial metrics', below).

- **Cost of sales:** This is the direct costs you incur in producing and/or delivering your product or service. Consider the costs that are associated with producing the product or delivering the service (such as raw materials and labour costs). These are often variable costs that fluctuate with revenue.

- **Operational costs:** This includes all the expenses not related to production. They will include

how much you spend each month on admin,
sales, marketing, legal fees, rent, overheads,
management salaries and probably several
other types of cost particular to your type of
business. It's often easy to miss some costs such
as recruitment fees or costs of training new staff.

Knowing where you need to focus is one thing, but
it's often difficult to know where to start when it
comes to applying this in practice. There's nothing
worse than a blank spreadsheet. That's why we've
created a free financial projection template over in
the free resources section of the Robot Mascot website
(www.robotmascot.co.uk/free-resources).

Cashflow summary

Your P&L forecast will record the income from a sale
in the month in which the sale was made. Equally, the
cost of an expense will be documented in the month
you plan to purchase the item. However, this fails to
take into account the actual flow of cash in and out of
the bank account. For example, you may have a 30-day
payment term on your invoices. As a result, while the
revenue is recorded in the P&L in month one, the cash
doesn't hit your bank account until (at least) month
two. The same principle applies to expenses.

When creating your projections, it's important to
include a cashflow summary so that you can demonstrate to investors that you're able to effectively

manage your cashflow and meet your commitments, such as payroll, every month. Showing how much cash you'll have available gives confidence that you'll be able to capitalise on any opportunities that come your way and have the resources available for any unexpected problems.

Balance sheet

Unlike the P&L and cashflow summary, the balance sheet details your business's net worth at any point in time. This is the document that shows investors the value of their equity and consists of three parts:

- **Assets**: Your assets are the things that your company owns and are split into current assets and fixed assets. Current assets include available cash and anything that could be converted to cash within a year, such as outstanding invoices and stock. Fixed assets are things owned by the company that are not expected to be converted into cash within a year, such as equipment, machinery and property.

- **Liabilities**: These are debts owed by the business: essentially, invoices owed to suppliers and contractors as well as loans, mortgages and taxes. As with current assets, there are current liabilities and long-term liabilities. Current liabilities must be paid within a year, while long-term liabilities will fall due more than one year from the date of the balance sheet.

- **Shareholders' equity (or net worth)**: This section of the balance sheet is how the document gets its name: where the sums balance. The company assets minus its liabilities must equal the net worth of the company. This total is the value of the shareholders' equity holding. Two types of equity need to be considered when forecasting net worth: *paid-in capital* – the amount of capital received via the sale of shares – and *retained earnings* – the profits that are to be reinvested back into the business.

As a minimum you should present investors with an opening and closing balance sheet for the first year after investment. However, I prefer to show investors a rolling balance sheet which forecasts the net worth of the business for each month throughout the five-year forecast period. Doing so demonstrates that you understand your balance sheet movements month by month, rather than just at one given point in time. This helps an investor better understand the developing trends over the period of the forecast, in the same way your P&L and cashflow projections do.

Key financial metrics

Investors will often quantify a good investment opportunity using key metrics that give them a snapshot of your current or projected performance. Below are the most common metrics that investors will look for when assessing your investment opportunity:

- **Annual recurring revenue (ARR)**: The proportion of each year's income that is expected to repeat year on year – these revenues are more predictable and ought to be more dependable than one-off sales

- **Gross profit**: The profit a company makes after deducting the cost of sales from revenue

- **Lifetime value (LTV)**: A prediction of revenue gained from the entire future relationship with a customer

- **Customer acquisition cost (CAC)**: The cost of turning a prospect (who may never have heard of you) into a customer (their money is in your account), including marketing and sales costs

- **Customer churn**: The average monthly loss of customers, typically in percentage terms

- **Burn rate**: The average rate at which cash in the business is decreasing

- **Margin**: The amount the product or service sells for above the actual cost of sale

You're able to calculate these metrics directly from the projection assets you've created. By documenting these key metrics in a financial summary and detailing some of them in your pitch, you'll be able to quickly communicate to investors the financial performance they can expect from your business, and why you make for an exciting investment opportunity. By saving investors from having to work these out for themselves you'll give yourself a competitive edge over other founders competing for the same pot of cash.

Summary

You now know about the three fundamentals of financial projections: *growth*, *speed* and *exit* and how to make sure your projections stack up against investor expectations. You've an overview for each of the assets that make up your financial projections (your P&L forecast, cashflow summary and balance sheet) and are aware of key metrics investors look at to assess your investment opportunity.

8

Principle Three: Structure

Having completed the Preparation phase of 'The Six Principles of the Perfect Pitch', we now find ourselves entering the Construction phase and considering the third principle: *Structure*. The structure determines which information from your business plan and financial projections is included in your pitch as well as the order in which you'll deliver this information to an investor. Without considering the structure you'll end up with a pitch that is difficult to follow and a business case that is almost impossible to comprehend, let alone invest in.

By the end of this chapter you'll learn why considering the structure of your pitch before you write any content is so important. You'll understand how getting the structure right lets you unpack your idea in a logical and investor-friendly way. You'll also learn the biggest mistake that I consistently see entrepreneurs make when creating their pitch structure, and you'll be introduced to the five acts of the perfect pitch, a method you can use to craft a compelling and memorable presentation.

Why structure is important

The structure of the pitch is vital, it's what helps an investor easily digest all the information about your business in a way that is logical and easy to understand. A good structure should take the investor on a journey of discovery. It's like the plot of a good novel. You probably wouldn't begin a novel with the ending, but you certainly would start writing it with the end in mind. In fact, before you write anything, you'd consider the whole plot from beginning to end – thinking carefully about the journey you want to take the reader on.

That's exactly how this book started: with a structure. I considered all the things I wanted to tell you about becoming an investable entrepreneur, and the order in which I need to tell them so that this book makes sense to you. There would be no point in me jumping into 'The Six Principles of the Perfect Pitch' without first making sure you understand the foundations – elements like the fundraising journey, the key fundraising assets and the purpose of a pitch have all given you vital context. Equally, it's no good me stopping at 'The Six Principles of the Perfect Pitch' and leaving you without any knowledge of how you go about getting these fundraising assets in front of investors.

The structure of your pitch is important for three reasons:

1. It will help you effectively break down the narrative into digestible chunks, keeping your text pithy and to the point; this will help no end during principle four: *Content*.

2. It will help investors navigate your pitch and better absorb the information about your idea, business case and market.

3. It will ensure your pitch demonstrates the three elements of being an investable entrepreneur (that you're highly resourceful, understand the financial risks and have a plan for commercial success).

When it comes to planning your structure it's important to understand that 80% of angel investors describe themselves as 'sector-agnostic'. This means that you should assume the investors are not experts in your niche and will know very little about the particular sector in which your business operates. In addition, it's also safest to assume they'll know almost nothing about your business itself.

The structure, therefore, is key to building up an investor's knowledge of both your business *and* the market or niche in which it operates. It's therefore important that each slide builds upon the information given in the slide before, so that the investor can go from knowing nothing about your business and market, to understanding enough to make a judgement on whether or not they're interested in pursuing investment – all in around four minutes. Most of us spend longer than that deciding what to have for dinner.

The biggest structural mistake

Creating your structure is much like planning the delivery of a new university course. If I were creating a new physics degree, I wouldn't start lesson one, semester one, with an advanced topic like string theory. I'd need to build up your knowledge of the basics of physics first. Each lesson would build upon the lesson before, until you have the knowledge required to comprehend the concept of string theory.

The same is true for your pitch. If you don't consider the structure as a journey of discovery, you often fall into the trap of assuming the investor knows what you mean before you properly explain it. It's a common problem. I'll often see a pitch refer to something in slide one or two that isn't fully explained until perhaps slide ten of the pitch. While reading slide two, investors have no idea what is being referred to – because they haven't seen slide ten yet. You do, it's your business. But the investor may know nothing of your business yet. When they get to slide ten, they may well join the dots and make the connection. You can get away with something like this if it happens just once or twice. The investor can make the connections and keep up. It's annoying, it won't help your cause, but they do manage.

However, what I see on a daily basis are pitch decks that have this occurring multiple times throughout a pitch. There's constant back and forth and it's impossible to keep up and take it all in. The worst thing is, most founders don't even realise that they're making this mistake, even when you tell them. They'll go and revise the deck in an attempt to restructure it, often without any success.

The problem is that they're too close to the business. It can be really hard as a founder to take yourself outside your business and into a mindset where you can see your business case from the perspective of someone who knows nothing about what you do, or how you do it. It's equally hard to consider your pitch from the perspective of someone without your sector expertise, market knowledge and all the research and life experience that has led to your creating this incredible business idea.

However, don't think that this means you should follow a rigid, pre-determined, paint-by-numbers structure. Google 'what should I include in my pitch deck?' and you get more than 32 million results. Many articles give a different interpretation of what you should include in your pitch. Some offer a structure that has worked at raising substantial investment for the author of the article: but this doesn't mean it's right for you.

The truth is, your business is unique. It therefore requires its own, unique combination of slides that will best tell your story to investors and construct a logical and investor-friendly narrative. Just ten different articles consulted after the Google search I mentioned identified over thirty different slides that would provide you with 'the perfect pitch structure'. Now, considering the rule of thumb that your pitch should be between 15 and 20 slides, it would be ridiculous to prepare 30 different slides for your pitch, even if you want to keep a few up your sleeve – for difficult questions.

Accordingly, you will need to decide which information you should include and which you shouldn't. This will largely be informed by the two sets of assets completed in the preparation phase – your business plan and financial projections. By considering which elements are the most powerful and persuasive parts of your business case, you can begin to form a structure that shows your investment opportunity in the best possible light.

The five acts of the perfect pitch

Much like writing a film script or a play, you can consider your structure as a series of 'acts'. The five-act structure is a popular method of doing this, and has been for a long time. Originally used by the ancient Greeks, the five-act structure guides an audience through a story by creating tension and drama. Shakespeare was a big fan, and it is a structure still used for many films and plays.

Traditionally, the five-act structure consists of exposition, rising action, climax, falling action and the resolution.

1. **Exposition**: This sets up the story and provides context. Most importantly, it contains the inciting moment, from which the story starts.

2. **Rising action**: This presents obstacles, which the main characters have to overcome. These obstacles hinder their progress and stop them reaching their goal.

3. **Climax**: This is the turning point of the story. It marks a change, for better or worse. It's the moment of highest tension.

4. **Falling action**: By now, the main part of the story has finished, and you find yourself heading to the conclusion. It's a steady calm after the tension of the climax.

5. **Resolution**: This is the resolution of the story, where the loose ends are tied up and the narrative concludes.

Now all this talk of creating tension and climax may sound a little dramatic for a pitch, and that's because it is. It's a structure for creating high drama and high tension in plays and novels. But you can apply a five-act structure to your pitch. I've created the five acts of the perfect pitch specifically for this reason and I'm going to share them with you now. The five acts are: the hook, the essence, the evidence, the plan and the ask.

THE FIVE ACTS OF THE PERFECT PITCH

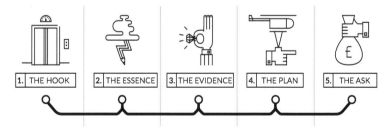

1. **The hook**: Here your sole purpose is to get investors excited about your big idea. You'll do this by showing them the most powerful

or emotive angle from which to consider your business.

2. **The essence**: Here you'll set the scene and give the investors an overview of your business. By the end of the act they need to understand what you do and why you do it.

3. **The evidence**: This is the climax. It's where you deliver the killer blow. You must prove that your product is in demand using the evidence you have gathered from your product/market fit experiments.

4. **The plan**: Here you show that you have credible plans for future business growth, have fully understood the financial risks involved and have plotted the route to success.

5. **The ask**: Finally, you want to persuade the investors to act. You may ask directly for the amount of investment you're seeking, or give details of how to get in touch to discuss the investment opportunity further.

In all five acts you should refer to your business plan and financial projections, to ensure the structural elements you put in place are the strongest parts of your business case. This is why one-size-fits-all structures don't work. They can force you to pitch the worst or most irrelevant parts of your plan. By considering your structure in five acts you'll only ever present the most compelling parts of your business case and in doing so you'll position yourself as an investable entrepreneur.

Summary

In this chapter you've learned why the structure of your pitch is so vital. You understand that getting the structure right lets you unpack your idea in a logical and investor-friendly way. You understand that different businesses need different pitch structures, and you know how the five acts of the perfect pitch can help you craft a compelling and memorable presentation.

9

Principle Four: Content

If creating the pitch structure is akin to developing the structure of a play or novel, then the content stage is like writing each individual scene or chapter. It's at this stage that you'll go into the detail of each slide, decide what information from the business plan goes in and what isn't relevant. You'll consider the hierarchy of the information and then produce written content that expresses the information in a compelling and engaging way.

This chapter isn't intended to be a manual on copywriting. There are loads of great books out there for that. Instead, I want to talk to you about the tried and tested process we use at Robot Mascot to produce clear and compelling slides. By the end you'll understand the two core styles of slide content and be able to determine which content to include. Finally, you'll take away some tips on how to write articulate and compelling content for your pitch.

The two core slide styles

As with structure, there's no one-size-fits-all approach for slides. Of course, there are good starting points for constructing certain types of content and basic templates can easily be found from a Google search. These may serve as a useful starting point; however, my recommendation would be to avoid spending too much time looking at templates and example pitch decks during this stage as they limit your ability to think openly about how best to communicate your own individual message. Remember that no business is the same, so what worked for Airbnb, Uber or Facebook is unlikely to work so well for your business. This is why template approaches are unable to deliver the same, consistent results as this methodology.

Before we jump into how you'll create clear and compelling slides, you first need to understand the two different types of slide you will be building your pitch out of: narrative slides and informative slides.

Narrative slides

Narrative slides explain a concept or set up an argument. Slides that introduce your business idea, such as problem and solution slides, are led by narrative. A narrative slide is the best way to sell an idea and bring the audience on board with your concept. You'll typically find narrative slides in the first three parts of the structure: hook, essence and evidence (see Chapter 8).

Unlike writing a novel, which would typically have a beginning, middle and end, a narrative slide typically has just a *beginning* and an *end*. It takes a bit of practice, as this goes against everything you'll have been taught at school about writing, but trust me, it works for delivering a powerful pitch.

A narrative slide works with what I call a 'set-up and score' formulation. Like playing volleyball, the purpose of this content is to first set up the shot, then smash it home to score a point. Your content should start by setting the scene, before hitting your point home with a punchy and convincing argument. One example is this narrative slide that Robot Mascot produced for our client WleePay (a mobile-money app bringing banking to millions in rural Africa):

AFRICA'S MOST COMPREHENSIVE MOBILE-MONEY APP

For the first time, rural Africans can easily and effectively manage all forms of banking with just their mobile and without the need for physical cash.

WleePay will be Africa's most complete financial services application.

In some cases, one set-up may score multiple times and deliver a series of arguments: such as this problem slide that we created for our client Web3 Labs (a commercial solution for building, launching and operating blockchain applications):

ESTABLISHED BUSINESSES STRUGGLE TO ADOPT THE DISRUPTIVE POWER OF BLOCKCHAIN

- Blockchain is a niche technology that requires considerable expertise.
- Training existing developers in blockchain is time-consuming.
- Blockchain developers are in short supply and are expensive.
- Blockchain application monitoring is challenging even for experienced teams.

You'll notice in these examples the set-up is an engaging headline and, in the case of WleePay, a one sentence introduction. The 'score' is delivered by a sentence or series of key points that provide a compelling and memorable take-away for the investor.

Informative slides

Not every slide should be narrative led. Slides in which you explain key parts of your business plan are unlikely to fit this style. Slides that talk about your business model, deliver facts about your market or provide information (such as processes and timelines) are more suited to the informative style. You'll find this type of slide most often in the last three parts of your structure, evidence, plan and ask (see Chapter 8).

Unlike narrative slides, the informative slide provides a range of information that supports your big idea and demonstrates credibility. The difficulty when creating informative slides is getting the most relevant information across in the most concise and articulate way.

Typically, these slides will be set up by nothing more than a descriptive headline, followed by a series of key points or a collection of convincing information. One example is the content for this market opportunity slide that Robot Mascot produced for AerPart (an online marketplace for used jet engine parts that uses blockchain to secure and certify the history of every part, eliminating fraudulent and unsafe parts from circulation).

MARKET OPPORTUNITY

Total addressable market

$76 billion: The value of the global maintenance, repair and overhaul (MRO) market (2017)

Service available market

$48 billion: Global MRO spend on engines and components (2017)

Service obtainable market

$160 million: AerPart market share (1% of EU and MENA regions)[10]

Another example is this business model slide we created for Highland Powerhouse (the world's first vegetable oil power station):

BUSINESS MODEL

Electricity suppliers pay us for each kWh we produce up to a pre-agreed production level.

13p	Income per kWh
5,000 kWh	Hourly energy production
£5.7m	Annual revenue

Unlike narrative slides, which follow the 'set-up and score' format, an informative slide is led by the information you're trying to convey. It's often the case that this information will be turned into some kind of visual or diagram in the design stage (more about that in Principle 6: Design). So, it's important to try and think visually when writing this type of content (sketching out or imagining how the information could be portrayed visually can really help the process of writing this type of slide).

---

10   MENA stands for Middle East, North Africa.

Step 1: Deciding the content

Once you know which slide format you're dealing with for any given slide, the first step is to decide which content from your business plan is most relevant to building your business case to an investor, and which is not. Each slide should have its own focus and talk exclusively about one element of your business plan.

As with the structure, it can be hard to know what the most important things are when your head is in the business. It's important, therefore, to consider what an investor wants to know to make the decision to invest in you. Go back to Chapter 3 and recap on the mind of an investor if you need to.

The best way to decide which content to include in each slide of your structure is to go through each relevant section of your business plan and highlight what you think are the most important parts. Once you've compiled a shortlist of the most relevant and compelling information for each slide, reduce this further to the most inspiring arguments.

I mentioned in Chapter 6 that at Robot Mascot we created our PitchPrep platform because of the difficulties we found in getting adequate information from our client's business plans. The other key purpose of PitchPrep is to draw out all the compelling reasons why our client's idea exists so that we can create an inspiring narrative of what they do and why they do it. We developed this part of the platform after realising that founders often find it really difficult to tell their story. Even with an unlimited word count, or a four-hour workshop to tell us about their idea, founders would often miss important insights that would compel investors' attention. And it's not just us who've noticed it, over 80% of investors I speak to say the most frustrating thing about receiving pitch decks is not being able to understand what the business idea is, or why it even exists. By thinking about the key insights needed to create an inspirational narrative you too will be able to influence an investor's thinking.

Step 2: Constructing a communication hierarchy

Once you have a shortlist of content, the next step is to begin considering the order in which that information appears on the slide. We call this the communication hierarchy. It's a process of strategically placing the content in a defined order so that the information on each slide is delivered in a logical, and engaging way. For example, some information is more important than others and you may therefore think it should be the first thing the investor reads on the page. In other cases, less important information has to be first in order to provide context to the main content.

Getting this part right is vitally important, as the communication hierarchy has a massive impact on how investors are able to absorb the information. Get it wrong and your message will be muddled, and investors will be confused.

Step 3: Writing the content

To ensure the content is compelling, each slide will need to communicate to investors in two ways. First it must *justify* something about your idea, then it must *engage* the investor. Your justification will most likely explain *what*, *why* or *how* you're doing something. You'll engage investors by using content that is based in either *logic* or *emotion*.

Your job at this stage is to take the draft content of the slide and consider which angle you'll focus on. Having this focus will help you create much more concise content. For example, one slide may focus on *what* problem you're solving and support the case using *logic*. If you also tried to include *why* now is a good time to solve the problem using an *emotional* angle, you'd muddy the communication. If you feel both are important to building your business case, you'd be better making these points on two separate slides.

For example, the content Robot Mascot created for our client Frolo (a social networking app for single parents) talks about *what* the problem is, but delivers it using an *emotive* angle:

SINGLE PARENTS EXPERIENCE PARENTHOOD DIFFERENTLY TO THOSE IN A RELATIONSHIP

Single parents can often struggle with:

- Loneliness and isolation
- A lack of support
- Mental health struggles
- Difficulties managing the politics of co-parenting
- The stigma of being a single parent

In comparison, this pitch for Upside (a FinTech platform enabling consumers to save automatically by using artificial intelligence to find savings and cashback from their everyday spending) uses *logic* to define *why* now is a good time to solve the problem:

PEOPLE ARE STRUGGLING TO SAVE

- UK saving ratio has been at an all-time low since 2017.
- A total of 9.79m households in the UK have no savings.
- 3.5m households have less than £1,500 in savings.

- 5.8m people in the UK earning £30,000+ are low savers (have less than £1,500).
- Current financial habits leave households at substantial risk in times of crisis.

In addition to the above you'll also need to consider the following when writing your content:

1. **Length**: Keep slides short and to the point. You'll notice that not a single example I've shared in this chapter exceeds 75 words. Most are under 50.

2. **Tone**: Overly flamboyant advertising speak should be avoided (your pitch isn't an advertising campaign) and everyday language should be used so that it can be easily understood.

3. **Jargon**: Remember, 80% of investors are not experts in the sector in which they are investing, so they're unlikely to understand your industry terminology.

Summary

You now know the two core styles of slide content (narrative slides and informative slides). You understand that to create a compelling and engaging pitch you must first determine which content to include in the slide, before deciding the communication hierarchy to ensure the greatest impact. Finally, you know that to ensure your slides are compelling and articulate you should write content that focuses the communication on just one justification (what, why or how) with one engaging angle (logic or emotion).

10

Principle Five: Clarity

We're now approaching the end of the construction phase and the fifth principle: *Clarity*. The clarity stage is all about further refinement of the text. It's where you review all the content. Each slide is considered, both in insolation and as part of the overall structure. It's important to ensure that every word has a purpose, and that the chance of misinterpretation is identified and dealt with.

In this chapter you'll learn about the vital importance of the clarity principle and why it has such an impact on your chances of securing investment. You'll know how to ensure your pitch is clear, concise and compelling and you'll discover the most common mistakes that you should avoid when checking the clarity of your pitch content.

Clarity is king

You may feel like skipping this stage. Once you've completed the content, you'll most likely think that you've nailed it and be excited to jump into designing your deck. You've probably got some investor meetings and pitch events lined up and you're rushing to get your pitch finished in time. However, it's this stage that can make or break your pitch. A lack of clarity will kill your chances of investment. If you don't complete this stage, you may as well cancel those investor meetings, and go for a drink instead of turning up to that pitch event. Without a further refinement of the content your pitch will not have the impact you were hoping for; you'll waste your time, disappoint potential investors and throw away your chance to raise some much-needed capital.

Even the experienced copywriters on our team need to go through the clarity stage, and they write investment pitches for a living. Day in, day out they produce content for an ever-growing range of business ideas, from blockchain to artificial intelligence, from nutritional supplements to social networking apps. They're masters in pitch structure and content, but even these professional copywriters need some support to achieve ultimate clarity. It's easy for even the most experienced copywriters to get blindsided by the complexity of a business, once their head is deep in the business model. So, to deliver the best results for our clients, we always ensure that a second member of the team assesses the output from the structure and content stages for clarity. By having this completed by someone other than the original copywriter we can ensure that the pitch content delivered is clear, concise and compelling.

BALANCING BREVITY AND DETAIL

Every founder is different; and each stage of this methodology will feel more natural to some than to others. Some find the Preparation Phase tough, while others will struggle with parts of the Construction Phase. I remember fondly working with one of the most detailed founders I've ever met. He was launching a pre-seed round of funding for his FinTech business. Ahead of our working together he presented me with his investment materials. They were like nothing I'd ever seen before. He had a 123-page business plan, and a 66-slide pitch. It's still by far the most impressive and detailed strategy I've seen from an early-stage founder.

None of the content was bad. It was well written, and it was abundantly clear that he really knew his stuff. All the key elements of the structure were there, and he had the insights, the research and the strategy that would lead anyone to believe he was going to succeed. His single biggest weakness was achieving clarity; and he knew it. It's the only reason he wanted to work with Robot Mascot and go through 'The Six Principles of the Perfect Pitch' with us. Specifically, for this step in the process.

The trouble wasn't that he didn't know what to say or had glaring holes in his business plan or financial projections. His problem was that he had too much knowledge, too much experience and had done too much research. He had so much great stuff that he was struggling to succinctly communicate what he offered to investors. He was obviously talented, but every investor walked away so overwhelmed with information that they didn't know what to think.

Investors and entrepreneurs should work well together. Investors are looking to deploy capital into something that will grow their wealth and entrepreneurs are looking to turn that capital into returns that massively outperform all other forms of investment. Yet entrepreneurs with incredible potential find themselves on the scrap heap before their journey has even begun. And it's all down to lack of clarity.

Ensuring your pitch is clear, concise and compelling

I like to think of this part of 'The Six Principles of the Perfect Pitch' as like panning for gold. It's your opportunity to remove all the unnecessary silt, only to be left with the golden nuggets. The clarifying process is similar to the role of an editor in the production of a novel. Like a good editor you'll need to go back over your pitch and:

- refine what you're trying to convey

- focus the impact of your narrative

- trim your text as needed

- improve the pace and rhythm (remember setup and score?)

During this stage you should be assessing your pitch by considering both the overall structure and narrative of the deck, and the individual slides. This is your opportunity to reconsider the structure now all the content is in place, as well as revisit the hierarchy and content for each slide. I would strongly recommend that you take a break from the pitch content for a couple of days or so and then go through this process at least twice.

Step 1: Ensure your content is clear

This is all about ensuring your content can be easily understood by anyone who reads it, regardless of their background and experience. Many angel groups, investment funds and VC firms use interns and juniors to filter pitch submissions, so it needs to be easily understood by all. Do a final check for jargon and buzzwords – because they form part of your everyday vocabulary you can often end up using them without realising.

For example, when explaining our client Coolbytz' product, the Robot Mascot team could have expressed it in the following way:

THE INDUSTRY CAN BE AUTOMATED

- We are a digital transaction broker between customers and suppliers in the technology sector.
- We provide an ecosystem that seamlessly meshes between providers, saving costs through efficiency.
- Proprietary technology achieves a state-of-the-art bespoke and unbiased platform for buying and selling.
- An immediate platform resource avoids lag.
- Buying and selling IT digital products and services is no longer prosaic but future-proof.

Instead, we wrote:

AUTOMATION OF IT AND DIGITAL SERVICE PROCUREMENT

- Simulates real-time performance for precise decision making
- Enables safe buying and selling of services at scale
- Simplifies and streamlines the whole procurement process
- Provides data and insights for informed decision making

Now that you can read your pitch with all the content in place, it's also worth taking a step back and looking again at your pitch structure through the eyes of someone who knows nothing about your business. This will help you determine whether or not your business case is presented in a clear and logical order.

Step 2: Ensure your content is concise

Being concise is the art of creating content that is brief yet comprehensive. It improves the reader's ability to understand what you are saying, while giving more flexibility and freedom to create an engaging design in the final stage. It's important to ensure there is a balance between brevity and detail. To do this it's worth checking what information the reader has already learned from the previous slides and avoid repeating it (other than for dramatic effect). Charts and graphs can turn complex paragraphs into succinct information. Double-check the length of the text on each slide and aim for less than 50 words (you may be able to restructure sentences to keep the same meaning with much fewer words).

For example, we could have written this elevator pitch for our client BoMaDU (a FinTech product for first-time buyers):

TRANSFORMING FINANCIAL SUPPORT FOR FIRST-TIME HOMEBUYERS

An industry culture of cautious lenders, ever-increasing deposits and a rapid rise in house prices across the UK, is making it increasingly difficult for first-time buyers to get on the housing ladder. With the gap between mortgage offers and the purchase price of homes widening, saving for a house deposit is harder than ever.

We enable first-time buyers to get on the property ladder with fair, ethical and smart deposit funding for first-time buyers. Providing the helping hand needed to get a deposit together in a simple and affordable way.

Instead, we wrote:

DEPOSIT LOANS FOR FIRST-TIME HOMEBUYERS

An increasing gap between first-time buyer mortgage offers and the purchase price of property is making deposits harder to obtain.

We enable first-time buyers to get on the property ladder with fair, ethical and smart deposit loans for first-time buyers.

Step 3: Ensure your content is compelling

Compelling content is what keeps the reader engaged and wanting to know more. It's what gets remembered after an investor puts the pitch down, and what investment analysts excitedly share around the office. Your content may be clear and concise, but if it's not compelling you'll be easily overshadowed by another pitch. You should ensure each slide has one key takeaway that you want the reader to remember. This could be a statistic, an overall feeling or a conclusion they draw. Also, check that each slide has *either* an emotive *or* a logical angle, as discussed in Chapter 9, and ensure that your whole pitch has a healthy mix of both.

For example, we could have written this vision slide for our client ADL Estate Planning:

OUR VISION IS TO BE A LEADING PROVIDER OF ROBUST INTEGRATED WEALTH PROTECTION AND INHERITANCE PLANNING, DEVELOPING ETHICAL PROJECTS ACROSS THE UK

The goal of ADL is to provide clients with the peace of mind that their financial affairs are being looked after by a fully qualified financial advisor, with their best interests at heart. And, as a leading ethical financial advisor, we will generate the revenue to create projects with positive social impact throughout the UK.

Instead, we created a statement that had impact and appealed to both the head and the heart:

OUR VISION: TO BE THE UK'S MOST ETHICAL FINANCIAL ADVISOR

As a leading provider of robust, integrated wealth protection and inheritance planning, we will not only look after the interests of our clients but also generate revenue with which to create and support social impact throughout the UK.

The most common mistakes

Clarity can be the most difficult stage of the process. We're often talking fine margins; a sentence cut here, a few words replaced there. But bear with it, because it's what makes all the difference. Removing the fluff is the hardest part. But it's well worth it, come the end of the process.

We've observed many startups approach the issue of clarity for themselves in a number of different ways, not all of them with great success. I thought it would be useful to share with you some examples of founders thinking they are helping matters and improving clarity but ending up doing the complete opposite.

Asking friends and family

While this group of people are great for raising your first round of investment, they're useless for getting feedback on your pitch; pretty much for the same reasons. They love you; they don't want you to fail; and they're afraid to offend you. All extremely useful traits when looking for a few grand to keep the dream alive, completely useless when asking for their honest feedback on your pitch. Sure, they'll spot some spelling mistakes, but they're unlikely to give you the hard-hitting feedback you need.

Asking other founders who've never raised investment

There are two types of founder: those who have raised investment and those who haven't. Those who haven't are not qualified to pass judgement on your pitch content. They've never successfully convinced an investor themselves, so they're not the best source of information. As friendly as the other founders are in your co-working space, don't end up co-creating your pitch with them – what was once quite clear will quickly descend into a mangled mess of differing opinions.

Asking investors

Trust me, unless you've had a long personal relationship that pre-dates your need for investment, asking investors for feedback is a sure-fire way to wind them up. It's enough to keep on top of the hundreds of unsolicited LinkedIn messages asking for investment, without also having to provide a free assessment service. And anyway, they're not communication experts; they're unlikely to be able to give you pointers on how to improve the clarity of your message. Rather, they'll just tell you they don't get your idea and you need to improve your pitch.

Using bold text

I see this a lot, and it really frustrates me. Rather than taking the time to consider the content and reduce and refine the message so that it's clear and concise, many founders simply go through their deck and , in long paragraphs, set certain words and phrases bold. While this action goes some way to telling the investor what you think is most important, you're leaving this critical content surrounded by unnecessary narrative – cluttering up the slide and making it harder for investors to get quickly to the crux of the business case in the few minutes they've set aside for reading your pitch. If you're riding the bold key, **please stop it** and go back to the start of this chapter.

Thinking questions are feedback

As you start pitching to investors, you're bound to be asked some questions. You can only put the highlights of your plan in your pitch, so it is inevitable that investors will want to know more. Don't assume these questions are feedback from investors that this information is missing from your pitch. It's tempting to go away from a pitch meeting and update your deck with answers to the questions you've just been asked. Sure enough, at the next pitch you're asked more questions, so you go back and update your slides again. Before long you're back where you started, and your pitch is long, cluttered and confused. Once you've completed your pitch, stick with it. Expect to be asked questions, be happy to cover them verbally and offer to send those asking a copy of your full business plan.

Increasing the number of slides

If you're unable to get across the information you want in one slide, the answer is not to split it into two. If you're struggling with this, it's because you're trying to either convey too much information or offer too much detail – in which case be brutal and cut some content. If you're struggling to cut your slides down to fewer than 75 words, you may need some professional help.

Summary

You now understand the importance of the clarity stage. You realise it can be tempting to skip this stage but now know that it's vital that you don't. You know how to ensure your pitch is clear, concise and compelling and you understand the common mistakes that you should avoid when testing your pitch content.

11

Principle Six: Design

W e're now entering the Create phase of 'The Six Principles of the Perfect Pitch' and our final principle: *Design*. You'll notice that the design of your deck itself is just one-sixth of the process involved in creating a convincing and compelling pitch. Yet far too many founders focus the majority of their time and resource on this stage. Of course, the design is vitally important (as I'll explain in this chapter) but don't for a minute think you can convince an investor without dedicating just as much effort to each of the previous five principles.

In this chapter you'll learn the power design can have over the way an investor perceives you and your business. You'll understand how you can use design effectively to better express your messaging, emphasise key points and affect the way investors consume the information. Finally, you'll understand the psychology of design and how that can be used to attract and convince investors.

The power of design

The design of your pitch is fundamental to the over-all communication of your message. Words, while incredibly powerful, are not enough, not when you need to express complex ideas in a matter of minutes. The design of your pitch materials can make all the difference between grabbing an investor's attention and being sent instantly to the trash.

Design is powerful for a number of reasons. Firstly, your brain is able to process images 60,000 times faster than text.[11] Think of a recent photo you saw on social media and consider all the information you gathered and remembered at a quick glance. After looking at the photo for just a few seconds you'll be able to recall who was in the photo, describe what they were wear-ing, the setting they were in, what they were doing and how they appeared to be feeling (sad, happy, angry etc). Now think about how many words you'd need to write to express the same detail in written form.

---

11   Harris Eisenberg (2018) 'Humans process visual data better', Thermopylae Sciences and Technology, www.t-sciences.com/news/humans-process-visual-data-better, accessed 5 August 2020

Suddenly, the idea that your brain processes images 60,000 times quicker than words is hardly surprising.

Not only this, but 90% of all information transmitted to the brain is visual.[12] This means your brain is particularly adept at absorbing and remembering visual information. It's why visual communication has always been, and always will be, the most compelling form of communication. That said, it also means our brains are bombarded with visual communication every second of every waking hour (as well as in our sleep if like most of the population you dream visually). It's therefore important that the design of your pitch has the necessary cut-through to stand out against the never-ending stream of bland, boring and ill-conceived presentations.

Ensuring the design has the right impact on your communication is nuanced. Consider these sentences: 'most of the time, travellers worry about their luggage' and 'most of the time travellers worry about their luggage'. The meanings are quite different, simply by the removal of a comma. Similarly, seemingly small changes in design can have a massive impact on the communication of your message. The size, style, colour and positioning of text, images and graphics can all have a strong impact on how your message is perceived. The goal for your pitch is to use the design to support your written text, giving emphasis and reinforcing the content of the written words.

12   Harris Eisenberg (2018)

Using design to communicate logically and emotionally

Design has been used throughout history as a tool to communicate a message. In fact, visual communication not only pre-dates the written word but also pre-dates the spoken word. Early humans were able to express their thoughts visually long before they became capable of speaking. Petroglyphs (images carved into the side of rocks) date from as far back as the Paleolithic period – over 700,000 years ago.[13] Not only could these early humans depict what they could see, but they also used visual communication to symbolise ideas and abstract concepts. Since the Stone Age, we have been using imagery to express ideas, and nothing has changed. The most powerful way to communicate your idea is still through visual communication.

Over time we have developed our ability to use visual communication to express ever more complex concepts and ideas: from the hieroglyphics of ancient Egyptians, to the first road map created by the Roman Empire, to the first complete visual atlas of the world from the late middle ages. However, it wasn't until the eighteenth century that we get our first example of modern information design. There are a number of great examples, but I want to share two particularly

---

13   Neil Collins (nd) 'Petroglyphs', *Art Encyclopedia*, www.visual-arts-cork.com/prehistoric/petroglyphs.htm, accessed 7 September 2020

powerful ones – both of which have specific relevance to creating a perfect pitch.

You may remember back in Chapter 9: Content, I explained how you must use language to communicate to an investor both logically and emotionally. Well, design can be used to the same effect.

Using design to communicate logically

In 1786, William Playfair, a Scottish engineer and economist, became the founder of graphical statistics when he invented several types of diagram – the line, area and bar chart for displaying economic data. A few years later, in 1801, he invented the pie chart.[14] Playfair was the first to apply geometry to the world of finance and in doing so completely changed the way we consume financial information. He was the first to recognise how visual depictions of financial data exploit our in-built ability to comprehend visual communication more readily than written information and how smart information design makes it easier for us to consume a large amount of complex information quickly.

Of course, the graphical devices Playfair invented are still in use today, and many more besides. His story is a great example of how by using information design

---

14 Ian Spence (2006) 'William Playfair and the Psychology of Graphs', *Proceedings of the American Statistical Association*, Section on Statistical Graphics, 2426–2436, www.researchgate.net/publication/228091928_William_Playfair_and_the_Psychology_of_Graphs, accessed 20 August 2020

techniques to express complex data we can make the experience of digesting and absorbing information much quicker and easier for investors. With the use of design, we can express what we want to say in a matter of seconds by demonstrating visually the point we are making in our pitch. Without the use of design, we would otherwise need to communicate the information in words or complex financial tables. These visual shortcuts allow us to provide much more information to an investor and do so in a way that resonates and is remembered.

Using design to communicate emotionally

Florence Nightingale is often considered the first to use information design for the purpose of persuasion. Unlike Playfair, who used graphics to depict data, Nightingale's Rose Diagram sought to convince people of the need for change.[15] She used the diagram to show the poor sanitary conditions of hospitals during the Crimea War. Her diagram formed part of a report that sought to expose the causes of soldier mortality in hospitals and bring about change in the British Army's approach to hospital care.

Nightingale believed that by showing, rather than telling, she'd be able to get across quickly, in an impact-

15   Hugh Small (1998) 'Florence Nightingale's statistical diagrams', paper presented at the Stats & Lamps Research Conference organised by the Florence Nightingale Museum at St. Thomas' Hospital, 18 March, www.florence-nightingale-avenging-angel.co.uk/GraphicsPaper/Graphics.htm, accessed 20 August 2020

ful way, that ten times more deaths had occurred from sickness than from battle wounds. Her design clearly showed how a British soldier was safer facing enemy fire than in a military hospital. As she started to raise funds for improved nursing care the money poured in, since people could quickly and clearly see the problem they were solving.

This is a great example of how design can have a massive impact on people's perception of new and alien concepts. If you remember, we discussed earlier how 80% of angel investors identify as sector-agnostic (their investment portfolio has no specialist focus) and therefore your idea, your customers' problems and your niche are all new concepts. By thinking like Florence Nightingale, you can give your pitch much more *gravitas* and communicate your message with much more force. By thinking visually about how you represent the emotive angles in your pitch you can create visual shortcuts to emphasise your point.

In most cases you should be using these techniques throughout your pitch material to better express the logical data and emotional storytelling of your pitch. Using information design to express logical information, such as statistics and financial data, is especially useful in the evidence, plan and ask parts of your structure. Using information design to communicate emotionally will most likely occur within the essence part of your pitch structure (see Chapter 8).

Using design to influence investors

The design of your pitch is crucial to gaining an investor's trust in you as an entrepreneur. As we've discussed, the correct use of design can dramatically alter the way we perceive information. The reason comes down to our natural and instinctive behaviours: something called our 'fight or flight' instinct. Humans are hard-wired to first perceive everything as a danger before it becomes known and trusted.[16] In everything we do we're constantly surveying our surroundings and assessing possible danger. For example, as we walk down the street we're constantly on the lookout for threats. We may not even realise it, but our brain is in overdrive identifying all the dangers we might face and whether we should remain where we are and overcome the threat or escape from it.

Our brains start by assessing what is closest to us, and then work through the field of view to the objects furthest away.[17] This makes sense: there is no point starting with dangers furthest away (and therefore of least risk) before you've addressed the most imminent dangers.

When your pitch lands in the inbox of an investor, you become an immediate danger. You're the nearest threat. Not an opportunity, but a threat. A pitch

---

16 Kevin Lynn Brown (2017) 'Visual design is all about fight or flight', *Medium*, https://medium.theuxblog.com/visual-design-is-all-about-fight-or-flight-4b198ba5a72c
17 Kevin Lynn Brown (2017)

landing in an inbox is essentially the same as you asking a stranger for money. To an investor you're just another founder sending them information about a business they've never heard of, operating in a sector they're unfamiliar with, asking them to part with thousands, if not millions, of pounds. The unfortunate truth is that, until you prove otherwise, you're a threat in the subconscious mind of even the most seasoned of investors.

It's for this reason that design is so powerful. The design is the first thing that resonates when they open your pitch. A well-thought-through design reflects well on you as the founder, it shows that you care about your business and instantly builds trust with the investor. But, most importantly, a good design will break down the barriers raised by the initial fight or flight reaction, it will allow you to lower the investor's guard and ensure that they are much more receptive to your message and that it is received in the way in which it is intended.

It's much the same as buying something online. I remember purchasing a romantic and luxurious spa weekend, so that I could propose to my now wife, Rachael. This was a big deal at the time, the biggest event of my life. It was a massive emotional investment. I wanted to take her to a boutique, independent spa rather than a national chain. As I searched and assessed the various options (all of which were previously unknown to me), my fight or flight mode was in overdrive. As I searched the web, I found myself gravitating towards the spas that had taken care and attention over the presentation of their facilities, had good imagery, good written communication and looked the most able to deliver on their promise.

Those with tired-looking websites and poor imagery felt uninspiring, untrustworthy and did not convey the impression 'luxury spa'. Of course, without booking a weekend at one of the shoddy-looking spas I'll never know whether or not I made the right choice. The chances are the experience and service would have been just as good, perhaps even better. But they missed out on the deal because they didn't inspire confidence in their ability to deliver on their promise – all from the way that they looked.

Summary

You now know that by properly considering and investing in the design of your pitch you can influence the way an investor perceives you and your business. You know that you can use design to support your messaging with powerful diagrams and graphics, provide emphasis to key points and influence how an investor consumes the information. You understand how getting the design right will ensure that your pitch stands out from your competition and will convince investors that you're a professional and trustworthy entrepreneur.

PART THREE

BEYOND THE PITCH

As with any marketing material, your pitch is no use sitting on the hard drive of your computer. You must have efficient and effective strategies to reach your audience, attract their attention and convert them into taking action. The same is true when seeking investment. Now you have your perfect pitch, it's time to find, meet and convince investors.

12

Preparing for your Investment Campaign

It always amazes me how few founders have properly considered what happens after creating their fundraising assets. Once they decide they're raising equity investment they plough full steam ahead into creating their pitch without even considering what comes next. As with any campaign, success lies in the preparation. With the excitement of having nailed your perfect pitch, it's easy to jump straight into seeking investors and signing up to pitch events. However, there are some critical steps you need to take before starting your investment campaign.

In this chapter you'll learn about the two additional assets you'll need in place on top of the pitch, financial projections and business plan in order to be campaign-ready. You'll also discover how you can beat the odds, make your life easier, complete your raise quicker and ensure your success is even more likely.

EIS/SEIS Advance Assurance

SEIS (the Seed Enterprise Investment Scheme) and EIS (the Enterprise Investment Scheme) are government-backed schemes that allow private investors to claim back 30% to 50% of their investment in high-risk companies against their tax bill. Having 'Advance Assurance' means that you've applied to HMRC ahead of closing your investment round and received provisional notification that investment in your business will qualify for the scheme.

EIS allows individuals to invest up to £1m annually and claim 30% of that figure as a reduction in their tax. They also pay no capital gains tax on any profit gained from the investment. Businesses are limited to raising £12m in total under EIS, with a maximum of £5m in any 12-month period.

SEIS allows an individual investor to invest up to £100,000 in a business and claim 50% of the figure invested as a tax break. As with EIS, the investor will be exempt from capital gains tax on any profit made from this investment. There is a limit of £150,000 on how much a company can raise via SEIS.

As you can imagine these schemes are incredibly popular with high-net-worth individuals and angel investors. There are plenty of upsides if the investment pays off, and while they still lose their money on those that fail, they have at least been able to reduce that loss through tax reliefs.

Some may see the schemes as benefiting the wealthy, but the two schemes mean the UK has become one of the countries with the highest quantity of private investments into early-stage businesses. Since their inception, the two schemes have encouraged over £20bn of investment into early-stage businesses[18] – stimulating our entrepreneurial sector and putting the UK at the heart of the global tech economy.

Having SEIS or EIS Advance Assurance will give you a massive advantage. With almost 40,000 investors claiming income tax relief through the EIS or SEIS each year it makes sense to offer this incentive to your potential investors.[19] Applying for the scheme is relatively straightforward; if you're struggling with your application, there are some great advisors out there that will be able to help you through the process.

---

18 HMRC (2019) 'Enterprise Investment Scheme, Seed Enterprise Investment Scheme and Social Investment Tax Relief, May 2019', https://assets.publishing.service.gov.uk/government/uploads/system/uploads/attachment_data/file/804455/May_2019_Commentary_EIS_SEIS_SITR_National_Statistics.pdf, accessed 7 September 2020

19 HMRC (2019)

There is one catch, however, and that is that you need the name of at least one investor on all applications. This often leads to founders finding themselves in a chicken-and-egg situation – you need to know who your investors are before obtaining Advance Assurance while the investors will often only commit to investing in you after you've obtained it.

However, the investors do not need to be 100% committed to your round when you apply, they merely need to have expressed interest. Once you've been approved you can change the name of the investors on your application at any time.

Legal documentation

To complete an investment round, you're going to need to have a range of legal documents in place. There are three core documents that you'll need. However, often many more legal documents are required that cover a range of matters such as IP ownership and employee share options.

> 'Once you have a meeting with an investor, they're going to ask you lots of specific details about your business structure. You need to be prepared to answer questions on things like IP assignment, founder share vesting schedule, company articles, EIS/SEIS compliance, and your cap table.'
> — Anthony Rose, founder, SeedLegals

This is where I have to make a confession. I'm not a legal expert, and I don't pretend to be. I highly recommend seeking legal advice from an expert as soon as you commit to raising investment so that you ensure both you and your investors are properly protected. Below, I outline the three key documents you'll need to discuss with your lawyer ahead of embarking on a fundraising round.

Term sheet

Once you've agreed in principle your terms with an investor (the amount they will be investing and the equity they'll receive in return) you'll need to create a term sheet. The term sheet records agreement between the parties and sets out the agreed terms. It should reflect the size of the deal and include details of the valuation, proposed levels of investment and any requirements for warranties (assurances of risk and liability) between the investor and the business owner. Typically, you'll agree a term sheet with a lead investor. This sets the terms on which subsequent investors will be able to join the round.

Shareholders' agreement

This document outlines the relationship between the new and existing shareholders once the investment has been completed. It addresses the rights agreed with the investors, such as any ability to appoint directors, receive information on the business and veto certain decisions taken at board level. It will also outline the autonomy of the founders to make particular decisions independently of shareholder approval, and contain the warranties agreed in the term sheet.

Articles of association

Typically, new articles of association are agreed on the completion of a funding round. This document will specify the regulations for your operations, management and administration. It lays out how tasks are to be handled within the company, such as appointing directors, holding board and general meetings, transferring shares and handling financial records. This document sits alongside the shareholders' agreement.

The idea of dealing with lawyers often concerns founders, especially in the early stages of business development. They're expensive, the answers they give might appear to bear little relation to the questions you ask and they seem to make life more complicated than it needs to be. However, LegalTech companies such as SeedLegals have built sophisticated technology to make the process as fast, simple and affordable as possible.

The approach for a successful campaign

In Chapter 4 I touched on the approach you need to take when creating a convincing pitch. That you should approach your investment materials as if they are sales materials. How, in the same way that a sales pitch tells your customers what to expect from the product or service they are buying, the investment pitch tells investors what to expect from your business now and in the future.

In much the same way, you should treat your investment campaign like a business-to-business (B2B) marketing funnel. After all, you are conducting a business transaction (remember, you are *selling* equity, not giving it away). Each party has something of value to exchange with the other. Just like any other marketing campaign the end result is an exchange of value.

As with any B2B sales cycle, getting to the final transaction can be a lengthy process. Unlike a consumer product, in business transactions the stages from raising awareness to purchase can take some months. A typical B2B sales cycle looks something like this:

- Identify need

- Draw up specifications

- Create a shortlist of providers

- Invite selected providers to pitch

- Negotiate details

- Make a decision

- Sign contracts

- Prepare the product or service

- Deliver the product or service

The typical process for achieving a commitment from investors is comparable:

	Typical B2B sales cycle	*Angel investor*
Stage 1	Identify need	Wants to protect and grow their wealth
Stage 2	Draw up specifications	Decide to invest in entrepreneurs, rather than the stock or property markets
Stage 3	Create a shortlist of providers	Receive pitches (up to ten per week); create a shortlist
Stage 4	Invite selected providers to pitch	Invite selected entrepreneur to a boardroom pitch (one per week)
Stage 5	Negotiate details	Negotiate details
Stage 6	Make a decision	Express interest; begin due diligence
Stage 7	Sign contracts	Agree term sheet (two per year)
Stage 8	Pay the invoice; product produced, or service started	Transfer the cash; receive the share certificate
Stage 9	Provider delivers the product or service	Founder delivers on promises

When you think of your investment campaign in terms of a B2B marketing campaign you put yourself in a much stronger position. You'll build a workflow that will enable you to keep track of leads and conversations, and create a campaign strategy that generates interest (I'll say more on this in Chapter 13).

Understanding that an investment campaign is very similar to the B2B sales cycle not only helps you formulate your fundraising strategy, but will also help set your expectations on the length of time it takes to raise investment. Just like a B2B campaign, it can be a long and drawn-out process.

When they first start raising investment most founders are under the illusion that the process can happen in a matter of weeks – and when you know the secrets contained within this book, it can. However, it's good for you to know that the average investment round takes up to six months to close. Knowing this allows you to plan your campaign accordingly and begin the process of raising investment so that you don't run out of cash before you're able to close your round.

Typically, you'll raise enough capital to last 18 months, so after 12 months you'll need to start thinking about the next investment campaign: before you run out of cash. If, because you've implemented the strategies in this book, you close your round early, then happy days – you'll accelerate through the fundraising journey quicker than planned, launch to market sooner than you anticipated and smash expectations.

The other consideration ahead of launching your campaign is the time you'll need to dedicate to executing it. Many founders who have successfully raised investment will recall how they spent the first few months trying to spread their time between bootstrapping their business and seeking investment. After getting nowhere for a number of months (and quickly running out of cash) they change their approach. They realise that, as the founder and CEO, they are responsible for top-level tasks (like fundraising) and not the day-to-day running of the business. Of course, in the early days you're CEO, receptionist, intern and everything in between. However, once founders realise that it is perfectly OK to stop all business development activity and focus instead on raising investment, they see a dramatic shift in results. They can manage leads better, pitch at more events and massively increase the number of meetings they have with investors. This is summed up perfectly by a Robot Mascot client:

> 'Everyone tells you raising investment is a full-time job, and they're right. When I was attempting to raise investment part-time, I was simply pitching at one or two events a week, hoping for investment to happen organically. I did that for about three months with no success. Then I had Robot Mascot rework my pitch and for the following three months I focused on investment

full-time. We raised all the investment within that period.'

> — Benjamin Carew, co-founder and
> director, WeCoffee

Beating the odds

Whatever you do, don't get overwhelmed by the idea of running an investment campaign alongside building your business. Yes, it's new. And yes, it's probably something you've never had to do before. However, if you apply what you're learning in this book, raising investment will be much easier for you than for almost all of your peers. By now you know how to ensure that you have the right assets to show that you're an investable entrepreneur, and you have a process for creating a convincing and compelling pitch. By the end of the next couple of chapters you'll also have the formulae for creating a campaign strategy that will put you months ahead of almost every other founder. This knowledge will put you much closer to the 1% who succeed than to the 99% who fail.

To set yourself up for success you should consider your investment campaign in these terms.

It's just a marketing campaign

Your fundraising campaign is nothing more than a marketing campaign. You're an entrepreneur; creating value and selling it is what you do. You know your business inside out, and you're confident in your idea (otherwise you'd be taking the easy life on a corporate payroll). You just need to turn your focus to selling shares, not products and services. As you'll see, the principles are the same, only the audience has changed.

Fundraising does not hold you back

The time you dedicate to fundraising does not hold back the development of your business, it accelerates it. If you don't raise investment, you'll never move through your fundraising journey at the speed you would like. You'll be forever trapped in the bootstrapping stage. This is the least enjoyable place on the journey. By putting a temporary pause on some development activity, you can quickly raise the capital you need, increase your valuation and rocket your business through the startup and scale-up phases.

It's actually quite simple

Over the years I've spoken to hundreds of founders and entrepreneurs, all of whom have had various experiences and various levels of success when it comes to seeking investment. Some are 19-year-olds that raised nearly £1m within three months. Others have secured millions off nothing more than a pitch, plan and projections (no proof of concept, no traction, no product). Over time I've seen patterns of activity that deliver results and, to be honest, none of it is complicated. It's these successful strategies that I'll be sharing with you over the final chapters of this book, so that you can invest in creating your perfect pitch, knowing that you've got the knowledge required to leverage it to its full potential.

Summary

You now understand the two additional assets you'll need in place to prepare yourself for your investment campaign. Applying for EIS and SEIS Advance Assurance will make you more attractive to investors, while having the necessary legal documents in place will allow you to capitalise quickly on commitments and protect both you and your investors after investment. Finally, you understand how by applying the strategies in this book you will make your life easier, your rise quicker and your success more likely.

13

Approaching the Right Sources of Investment

There are a number of different sources of equity investment for your business. We touched on them in Chapter 1 when we discussed the fundraising journey. Knowing the different sources of equity funding and considering the most relevant for your round is vital ahead of engaging in a fundraising campaign.

In this chapter I'll explain the most popular funding sources you'll encounter during the fundraising journey. You'll gain a detailed overview of each source of investment and learn more about the stages in which they invest, how much they invest per deal and their main aims for investing. By the end of this chapter you'll be able to select and approach your ideal investors.

Angel investors

Much of this chapter will be spent talking about angel investors. This is because, if you are reading this book, you're most likely in the startup or early scale-up phase of the fundraising journey. It's these phases in which angel investors are most prevalent, so they are your most likely source of investment.

Angel investors (or simply angels as they are often referred) are typically high-net-worth individuals who are looking to grow their wealth through investing in businesses. Much of the time angels come from a business background, so rather than putting their capital into the stock or property markets (something they know little about) they opt to back entrepreneurs – they understand how business works, and many are keen to serve on the board to help the business achieve its aims.

They tend to have less money to invest than their institutional counterparts, so to maximise their returns they are willing to take a higher risk by investing at an earlier stage of the company: typically, the pre-seed, seed and (more recently) Series A rounds. This is what gives them the name angels; they are the first serious investors in a business and will back you before anyone else considers you a good opportunity.

As the tech startup scene has established here in the UK we've seen a massive growth in angel investors;

but also, a large shift in their sophistication. After the 2008 recession there was a flood of angel investors into the market. They were drawing funds out of the volatile stock and property markets and (excited about the explosion of the UK as a world leader in the tech sector) they were turning to entrepreneurs. At that time, many seemed happy to invest in nothing more than a great idea that excited them. Nowadays, they are approaching their investment decisions much in the same way as an institutional investor. These once new and unsophisticated angels have got much wiser; they've learned what works and what doesn't.

The growth of angel groups has also had an effect on the sophistication of angel investors. In these groups, investors help each other assess the strength of a deal and share their knowledge. If someone is an expert in a particular niche, the others look to that person for guidance. If they invest, it's likely the other angels in the group will follow. These groups give new angels the advice and guidance they need to make smarter investment decisions, and level up their knowledge and sophistication.

'In my angel group, there's a structured due diligence process. Where someone in the group is an expert, they take the lead in that area. For example, a lawyer will head up due diligence on the legals. At the end of the process each lead angel will give the rest of the group their opinion.

There's a huge benefit in the collective thinking that comes from being part of an angel group.'
— Laura Harnett, angel investor

If you're to be taken seriously, you'll need to provide the same level of detail in your fundraising assets for angel investors as you would for an institutional investor. This means you'll need to invest more effort and more resources than you would have done five years ago.

To close your round, you'll often need to convince a number of angels to back your cause. The average angel invests in two deals per year at a value of £25,000 per investment.[20] So, to close a small SEIS round seeking to raise £150,000 the chances are you'll need six investors on board. Once you convince your first angel, however, closing your round becomes much, much easier. If one angel leads, others will follow.

The seven types of angel investor

In my experience, you can group most angel investors into seven different categories. As you up your networking and reach out to more and more high-networth individuals you're bound to meet some, if not all, of these characters.

---

20   British Business Bank (2018) *The UK Business Angel Market*, p 13, www.british-business-bank.co.uk/wp-content/uploads/2018/06/ Business-Angel-Reportweb.pdf, accessed 7 September 2020

1. The non-tech investor

They may not fully understand the technology behind a brilliant tech idea, but they will have plenty to say about the business model. They will form their own opinions on the strength of your business based on their vast business experience. Remember that, while they may not be *au fait* with the latest tech developments, they've most likely made a lot of money in business and know the ropes.

2. The eagle-eyed investor

After a successful pitch, they will scrutinise every aspect of your business plan and financial projections – so you'd better be confident that these demonstrate a credible and investable business model. They'll probably want to meet you several times and they'll execute heavily during due diligence. Anything you can do to make their lives easier – such as providing well-presented, detailed and easy-to-digest documents, summaries and reports – will go down well and show that you understand what they're looking for and can be trusted.

3. The follower

These investors are worth building a good relationship with. The only problem is that they want other angel investors to commit before they consider investing in your business. They'll never lead a round but are more than happy to follow a lead investor they trust. Once you have one of the other types of angel investor on board, circle back to these investors to see whether they're ready to join the party.

4. The insightful investor

Many angel investors don't just want to give capital: they also want to share their experience and expertise with a founding team that inspires them. They want to be a part of your success on a deeper level than just providing capital, often as a non-executive director, offering insightful advice and connecting you with people in their network who could accelerate your business.

5. The equity grabber

Not all investors agree with the first valuation that's brought to the table, and they may ask for more equity than you first proposed. There's nothing wrong with negotiating but take your time before signing any deals at a lower valuation. If you're consistently challenged over your valuation, be mindful that it could indicate that you're attempting to raise too much for your current stage in the fundraising journey.

6. The spent investor

Maybe they lost out on a few investments that didn't quite pay off; or perhaps they've invested further cash into a rising star in their portfolio. Either way, not all investors will have cash available to invest at the moment you approach them. They will, however, be accepting pitches as they want to keep their finger on the pulse. Remember that most investors have a network of other investors, so word of your opportunity will spread (if you build a good report you can even ask for introductions). Just be aware that they have no intention of investing money in you right now – but they might come good in later rounds, so keep them sweet.

7. The pessimist

These investors might show interest in your business model, but doubt you as a founder, which can understandably feel pretty personal. By demonstrating that you're an investable entrepreneur you should be able to alleviate those doubts completely. By having a believable business plan, credible financials and a perfect pitch you'll be able to convince even the most doubtful of investors.

Crowdfunding

The second most prevalent form of raising investment for those in the startup and early scale-up phases is crowdfunding. In fact, crowdfunding is responsible for investments large and small across all stages of the fundraising journey. As crowdfunding platforms have become more established, investors have become more confident in investing larger sums through these platforms. After VCs, crowdfunding platforms are the most active type of equity investment.

Crowdfunding uses the power of a network (the crowd) to make investing in your business easy. The platforms manage much of the technical and legal side of the deal in return for a small commission on the amount raised. This means that less sophisticated investors can invest without having to worry about the often-complicated process of closing the deal. Typically, people can invest relatively small amounts in your business – from a few hundred pounds. This makes crowdfunding a great option to leverage your personal networks and existing client base. Giving your customers an opportunity to own a small part of the company can massively increase loyalty to your brand.

Craft brewery BrewDog are one of the best-known success stories of crowdfunding. They've raised countless times via crowdfunding site Crowdcube and have used the opportunity to raise millions of pounds, achieve unicorn status and build a loyal fan base in the process.[21] Challenger bank Monzo made headlines when they achieved the fastest crowdfund ever, raising £1m in an incredible 96 seconds.[22]

The two largest crowdfunding sites in the UK are Crowdcube and Seedrs, whose merger was announced in 2020. You will need to be assessed by their team before you're accepted onto their platform. Like angel investors their analysts are looking for signs that your business has a credible plan and an investable business case. Unlike angel investors they're also looking for signs that your business has a strong community that would be likely to invest in you.

'In the early days, crowdfunding was centred more around raising capital and creating some PR buzz. Over the last few years, the game has changed. Community is now at the core.'
— Darren Westlake, founder and CEO, Crowdcube

It's also worth bearing in mind that almost all the top crowdfunding platforms will require you to have some initial investment committed to your round before you'll be accepted. So even if you feel you've a large enough network and audience to take full advantage

---

21 James Watt (2015) *Business for Punks: Break All the Rules – the BrewDog Way* (Penguin)
22 Tom Blomfield, 'Fastest crowdfunding ever: £1 million in 96 seconds', Monzo blog, 3 March 2016, https://monzo.com/blog/2016/03/03/crowdfunded, accessed 7 August 2020

of the power of crowdfunding, it's most likely you'll still need to convince some angel investors to back your business first.

Family Offices

A family office handles the investment portfolio of a high net worth family. They're typically in charge of assets well over £100m in value. Their main goal is to grow the wealth of the family so that it is protected across generations. It's likely they will diversify their portfolio across a range of investment assets such as stocks and shares, real estate, hedge funds, bonds and, of course, entrepreneurs.

Different family offices will have varying approaches, but (in the context of entrepreneurial investments) many are seen as somewhere in-between Angel Investors and Venture Capital firms. They may well invest in early stage opportunities but are just as likely to join with venture capital and private equity deals.

Family offices tend to be hard to identify, as you're often not dealing directly with the family office themselves. Instead you'll be communicating with their fund, which will most likely be set up as a separate company and will appear unrelated to the family office to an outsider. The investment fund you're dealing with will most likely look and feel like a VC, but instead of drawing their funds from a pool of different investors (known as Limited Partners in a VC), they draw their capital from a family fund. In some cases, different family offices may pool their funds together and invest through one umbrella entity.

Venture capital

This is often considered the first level of institutional investment. VCs are looking for businesses that have an established customer base, sustained revenues and are operating in a market in which a large injection of capital will achieve rapid growth and higher than average returns.

There are a number of active VC funds in the UK, well over 300 at the last count.[23] Typically, VCs invest in later-stage companies – those in the scale-up phase of the fundraising journey (raising their Series A, B or C+ rounds). They typically invest anything between £2m and £15m per deal and are looking for considerable returns – they often ask to see a path for a 150× return or greater on their investment before they are interested. Something founders often fail to understand is that each VC fund expects that almost all of its return will come from just one company. A couple will make a 5× return, a few will break even and the rest will fail.

---

23   Hannah Skingle (2019) 'Where are the UK's VCs located and where are they investing?', Beauhurst, www.beauhurst.com/blog/where-are-the-uks-vcs-located-and-where-are-they-investing, accessed 7 September 2020

The reality is that 97% of exit profits come from less than 0.1% of investments.[24]

THE VC POWER LAW

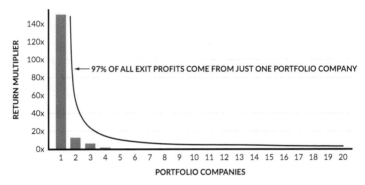

To qualify for VC investment, you'll need to be seen as a credible path to becoming the one business that will deliver that return. Everyone in a VC portfolio has to be seen to have that potential. If you cannot show that you have what it takes to achieve unicorn status, or you don't think that going down that path is right for you and your business, then a traditional VC investment may not be for you – angel investment, family offices or crowdfunding may be a better fit.

In recent years we've seen VCs backing fewer deals but at a much greater value, averaging just 450 deals

---

24 Adapted from J Engeström, 'What you should know about early-stage venture capital', Yes VC, 2020, http://bit.ly/WhatYouShouldKnowAboutEarly-StageVentureCapital

per year between all 327 VC firms since 2011.[25] This trend has led to a new breed of VC that is bridging the increasing gap between angel and VC investment. Funds like Seed VC help to incubate and accelerate early-stage tech businesses, before investing capital at the end of their programmes. This approach blurs the traditional lines between angel and VC investment. As the UK's startup ecosystem develops, we'll see more initiatives such as Seed VC take an institutional approach to early and mid-stage investment.

'Smart money is the future of investment. By delivering capital alongside deep operational expertise, funds like ours can support founders through the most crucial stage of their journey – increasing success and maximising returns.'
— David Reynolds, founding partner,
Seed VC

The process of applying to a VC is more formalised than dealing with an angel investor. Typically, your pitch will first be reviewed by an investment analyst (often a junior or intern). If it passes the initial checks, it's passed onto a senior analyst or investment manager for a more thorough review. If they like what they see, they'll invite you to pitch and if all goes well a few more meetings will follow. Once they're satisfied that you'll make a good investment, your proposal will be

25 Hannah Skingle, 'The most active UK venture capital funds', Beauhurst blog 6 September 2018, www.beauhurst.com/blog/most-active-uk-venture-capital-funds/, accessed 7 August 2020

taken to the investment committee (normally made up of the senior partners) for a final decision. In some cases, you may also be asked to pitch to the investment committee.

Private equity

I'll keep this brief as it's unlikely that if you're reading this book you'll be dealing with private equity (PE) firms any time soon. However, it's good for you to have an understanding of what could be on the horizon. Unlike VC funds (which look for mid-stage businesses with high growth potential), PE firms tend to invest in less risky, mature companies that are reaching the end of the scale-up phase – Series C onwards. They'll typically have a fund that is made up of a number of investments, and have set a predetermined value: once the fund has reached that value they'll close it and sell all the businesses within it to provide a return to their investors. PE firms will typically invest upwards of £50m in a single deal and can make a great exit opportunity.

Brokers and investor relations

The final source of funding that I want to bring to your attention is the use of brokers and investor relations agents. While not a direct source of funding themselves, they can be extremely useful to entrepreneurs.

Brokers are either firms, or individuals, that find potential deals for entrepreneurs. They can be a great option for founders who are struggling to find, meet and secure pitches with investors – or would rather spend time on their business than on chasing down investors. Brokers typically charge a success fee on any successful investment deals they introduce. Some will also charge a small retainer for their services. Because of this, many brokers and investor relations agencies will only work with entrepreneurs in the scale-up phase because they see businesses in the startup stage as more risky than what the investors they deal with are looking for.

Investor relations approach things more like a PR agency and less like having a 'little black book' or a database of contacts like a brokerage. Instead, they take on the responsibility for communications, marketing, investor-specific PR and sometimes even legal compliance to create effective communication between the founders and the investment community.

Summary

You now understand in detail the most likely funding sources you'll leverage during the fundraising journey. You've a particular understanding of angel investment, crowdfunding and VC funds, the three most popular sources of funding for pre-seed, seed and Series A rounds. You know when they invest, how much they invest and their main objectives for investing. You should now have the knowledge you need to effectively select and approach the sources of investment best suited to your business and have an understanding of the sources of funding you may need in the future as you move through the fundraising journey.

14

Implementing your Investment Campaign

By this point you have planned your fundraising journey, you know how much you're raising and how much equity you're selling in return, you've created the perfect pitch, you have your critical fundraising assets in place, you've been approved for EIS/SEIS Advance Assurance, you have all the legal documentation you need at hand and you know the different sources of investment you can approach. You're now ready to head out into the world and start convincing investors.

In this chapter I'll explain the importance of creating a campaign strategy and how by doing so you can dramatically increase the speed in which you raise investment. You'll learn how to target, meet and approach investors, and I'll share five tried and tested tactics that will help you lay the groundwork and put you in a strong position to convince investors that your business is the one to back.

The fundraising strategy

I've mentioned more than once in this book how seeking investment is nothing more than a specific marketing campaign. Everybody knows that to be successful in marketing you need a strategy. It's no good simply posting some uncoordinated content on Facebook, paying for some advertising, doing some PR and delving into direct mail without first considering how they all tie together and support each other to achieve the objective. The same is true when it comes to your fundraising campaign.

I've spoken to countless founders over the years who, armed with their pitch materials, excitedly head off expecting investors to fall over themselves to invest in their business. It just doesn't happen that way. Sooner or later these enthusiastic entrepreneurs realise that they've failed to put together a coherent strategy. By the time they've realised, most have wasted months which would have been better spent implementing their business plan.

Those founders who have a strategy in place seem to be much more successful, and in a much shorter timeframe. They've identified what they need to do, when they need to do it and the order in which they should do it. This allows them to accelerate their campaign with a laser-focused approach.

A fundraising strategy needn't be lengthy. It can easily be written on two sides of A4 paper. But it is necessary if you're going to have a clear and considered approach to raising investment. Spending a few hours mapping out your fundraising plan will save you months in your pursuit of an investor and create a competitive edge over your rivals.

A basic strategy should cover:

- **Investor targeting:** what type of investors will you focus on and who specifically will you approach?

- **Promoting your investment opportunity:** how will you create opportunities to get your pitch in front of investors?

- **Capturing and converting investor interest:** how will you capture and monitor investor interest?

- **A detailed action plan:** what will you be doing daily, weekly and monthly to find, meet and convince investors?

By outlining your plans in each of these areas you'll be able to run an effective and successful investment campaign. You'll have considered your approach and will quickly be able to tell what's working well, and what isn't. Having a fundraising strategy will deliver results quicker and mean you can sooner get back to what you love – growing your business.

Selecting and targeting the right investors

Many entrepreneurs will contact every single investor who comes up as a first, second and third connection on LinkedIn. They'll bombard every VC, angel group and fund that appears in the top ten pages of Google. And they'll be at every startup, pitch and investor event listed on Eventbrite. This is not how you go about successfully raising investment. Mass marketing hasn't been an effective marketing tool for decades. Focused and targeted campaigns are much more effective. And the same is true for founders seeking investment.

Rather than having broad messages that they send out to hundreds of investors, Robot Mascot clients have found much more success when they take the time to research investors, qualify them, identify those that are an ideal fit for the company and decide on an appropriate way to approach each selected investor. After all, this is a relationships game, not a cold, hard sell. By taking your time to identify and approach specific investors because you know they are a good fit for you and your business, you will have a much greater chance of persuading them to invest in it.

Successful founders typically start by discovering the sectors in which investors within their LinkedIn network (first and second connections) have invested in the past. Most of the time, angel investors will list this in their LinkedIn profile. VCs will usually list their portfolio on their website, and individual investment analysts typically list their specialist area in their bio. Once you're armed with this information you can create a targeted shortlist of investors that you need to approach.

Some founders decide to rank these investors from *most likely to invest* to *least likely to invest*, to gain a tighter focus. It's often best to start with the least likely investors, to refine your tactics and get some pitch practice in, before working up to the most likely investors.

Meeting and approaching investors

There are a number of ways our clients have met and approached investors effectively; the most common are networking, pitch events, on LinkedIn or via an introduction from a mutual connection. The method that almost every investor I know prefers is an introduction. Nothing beats a referral from a trusted third party. Before going in cold, exhaust all possibilities for getting a warm introduction. When meeting and pitching to investors at the bottom of your target list, consider asking them for introductions to other investors they know who may be interested in meeting you. If you've impressed them and have come across as investable, they'll most likely be happy to make an introduction, even if they don't think your business is the right fit for their portfolio. Hopefully, they'll be able to introduce you to someone higher up your target list – or to someone else not in your plan. Either way, this is a massive result.

Whichever contact method is used there is always one common thread that sees our clients achieve success, and that's making the approach personal. If you've completed the targeting exercise, then you'll know enough about the investor to make a personal approach. It's important here that the investor feels special, that they feel you've specifically chosen them because you see value in having a relationship.

> 'A warm introduction is the best. I'll always make time for a meeting if it's a warm introduction. But I still meet plenty of founders who have made contact through a LinkedIn message – as long as it's very specific and says that they are reaching out to me for a particular reason.'
> — Jerneja Loncar, founder, Good Tech Ventures

Getting a commitment from an investor will not be an overnight thing. First you make contact, then you pitch your business. Next, you'll have some meetings to further explore the relationship, test your resolve and deliberate over your business plan. Only once there is a trusted relationship between you both will a deal will be done.

How to make investors love you

Meeting investors can be daunting. You'll be very conscious of trying to make a good impression and will most likely feel desperate for them to like you and your business. With each pitch, however, it will get easier. Over the years I've identified a number of tactics that Robot Mascot clients have used to successfully build relationships with investors.

1. Show them the real you

After implementing 'The Six Principles of the Perfect Pitch', you're certain to have a convincing pitch. You'll also have a business plan that details the strategy you'll be implementing and financial projections that show the rewards on offer.

With these assets you'll be able to show you're an investable entrepreneur. But investors invest in people, not businesses: it's important that you also get across your personality when you pitch. They need to like you as much as they trust you. As tempting as it is, stay away from heavily scripted pitches. Instead, treat each point on every slide of your presentation pitch as a prompt, and expand on that point without notes. After all, it's your business, you know this stuff inside out. By keeping away from notes, you'll become much less robotic and come across much more naturally, giving investors a glimpse of the real you.

Additionally, when in boardroom meetings it's important to be authentic and honest with potential investors. If you've had failures in the past be upfront about them. You may have made a mistake early on in the business that cost you big time. The most important thing here is to show that you quickly learned from these mistakes and rectified them, putting your business in an even stronger position. Investors know you're not perfect. No one is. Do you think the investor sitting opposite has backed a winner every single time? Of course they haven't; sometimes they've made a mistake. Rather than have the investors dig around for the dirt, be upfront about it, own it and make it clear that you're great at learning and adapting to change.

2. Practice makes perfect

Your pitch looks and sounds great. It's clear, concise and memorable. But if you stand there in front of investors awkwardly looking at your feet with a noticeable quiver in your voice – you're not going to inspire confidence in your ability to inspire others to join you on your mission.

So, you'll need to practise your pitch. You'll need to practise it often. This doesn't include pitching in front of the mirror. Nor does it include pitching to friends and colleagues, for that matter. Doing so is a waste of time and doesn't simulate the real environment. Instead, attend pitching competitions, arrange your own events with your network, pull together people you don't know from your accelerator or office space and spend some time pitching to each other. Do whatever it takes but practise your pitch hundreds of times before you even start at the bottom of your target list.

Martin Luther King had given versions of his "I Have a Dream" speech on several occasions up and down the USA in the year previous to his famous TV broadcast. However, King had actually planned a different speech for the occasion. As he was delivering the broadcast, he 'started improvising a bit when he reached a sentence that felt clunky',[26] but after hearing his fellow activist Mahalia Jackson shout, 'Tell them about the dream, Martin!', he returned to what was, in effect, a tried, tested and rehearsed pitch. I doubt his first ever recital was anywhere near as impactful as this historic moment in front of millions around the world, but by opting for a tried-and-tested pitch his speech became one of the most famous and inspiring moments of all time.

---

26 Emily Crocket (2017) 'The woman who inspired Martin Luther King's "I Have a Dream" speech', *Vox*, www.vox.com/2016/1/18/10785882/martin-luther-king-dream-mahalia-jackson, accessed 4 September 2020

3. Treat investors as equals

It's easy for a founder to put investors on a pedestal and treat them as if they are some kind of higher being. After all, they have something you really, really want – large sums of money – and without these, your dream is dead. Or, at the least, it will be much slower and harder to achieve it. However, you must remember that they're just normal people, wanting to back an exciting entrepreneur and enjoy the successes it brings.

By treating an investor as an equal – another business mind as brilliant as yours – you don't bring them down, you raise yourself up. You'll find yourself in a more influential position and lay the groundwork for building a real relationship. Remember, you can offer something they want: high returns on their capital. And only you can deliver them this.

By approaching talks as an equal you actually come across more likeable and more businesslike. It subconsciously tells the investor that you're confident in your business plan and your idea, and that they're lucky to have the opportunity to speak to you about it – rather than the other way round. It's important to get the balance right, though; push it too far and the investors won't see you as an equal, but as arrogant and uninvestable.

4. Get out there

When it comes to raising investment, building relationships is key. Of the founders I've worked with, it's always those that are proactive networkers that have the biggest successes. They attend as many events as they can, they go to pitch events, meet-ups and build a community on social media – and they started doing this long before they had a fully prepared business plan or had completed their pitch.

These founders don't attend events in the hope of finding someone who'll invest in their business. Instead they slowly build up their network in the entrepreneurial, startup and investment scene so that, when the time comes to launch their investment campaign, they've a network they can leverage for warm introductions to their target list.

By building relationships with the mindset of 'finding people who may be able to help me' rather than the mindset of 'finding someone to invest in me' you don't come across as needy or desperate (trust me, investors meet more than enough needy or desperate founders). Instead, you're much more approachable, relaxed and genuine. It's amazing how many doors this will open. What's more, when you're not looking for investors, you'll almost certainly meet them.

Start networking now. Search Eventbrite and Meetup for some interesting events near you. Ask others at those events if they know of any other good ones and start getting yourself out there. Begin building your online community and social network. It will be worth the effort once you're ready to launch your investment campaign.

5. Build a tribe of investors

This one is my favourite tactic. I've saved the best for last. It's the culmination of everything we've talked about so far. It builds excitement and creates a desire to invest in you and your business.

If you've taken on board the first four tactics, you'll be a proactive networker, with a confident and natural pitch, who comes across as genuine and authentic. You'll have built a network of fans who are keen to help you and have begun building relationships with investors. As you maintain these relationships over time, you should keep your network up to date with your progress. This might be when you meet them again at the regular events you attend, or via an active social media strategy. Either way, your goal is to tell them of your successes and failures. Your goal is to be authentic; this means you have ups *and* downs. By sharing the low points (along with how you overcame these obstacles) you'll only add to your credibility. As you build deeper relationships you can begin to drop into the conversation that you'll be opening an investment round soon.

Before long, you'll have a queue of investors asking to be notified when you open your round. Pick a date in the future that gives you enough time to build a decent waiting list. While they're waiting send them your teaser pitch, telling them that you're putting the finishing touches to the full investor pitch, business plan and financial projections.

If your teaser pitch lives up to the hype you've created, they'll be keen to see the full investor deck and book a meeting with you to discuss the investment opportunity in more detail. As soon as you launch your campaign you'll be able to line up a number of meetings and pitch events in quick succession and rapidly close your round.

It's this tactic that led to one of our clients closing their round (and being offered nearly 50% more than they were asking for) after just one pitch.

Summary

You now know the importance of creating a campaign strategy and how by doing so you can dramatically increase the speed with which you close your round. You understand the importance of creating a targeted list of investors and understand how to meet and approach those investors. You realise that raising investment is all about building relationships, and not about the cold, hard sell. You also have five tried and tested tactics for making investors love you and laying the groundwork so that you can convince them that your business is the one to back.

15

Making it Happen

Y ou now have a blueprint for success. You understand the foundations of preparing the perfect pitch, and what it takes to become an investable entrepreneur. You have a methodology for creating pitch materials that will convince investors to back your business, and you have ideas and strategies on how to implement an investment campaign. All you need to do now is make it happen.

In this final chapter I'll set you on your way to becoming an investable entrepreneur. You'll learn the mistakes most often made by founders that mean that, even with all the knowledge, processes and strategies set out in this book, they still fail to secure funding, and you'll understand the traits that set an investable entrepreneur apart from the rest.

Mistakes you must avoid

Despite understanding the investment process, spending hours creating and crafting the critical fundraising assets and carefully considering their investment strategy, most founders still fail to raise investment. Why? Because they've made one of these mistakes.

Mistake One: Leave it too late

Too many founders consider raising investment when it's far too late. They don't leave enough time to properly consider their plan, produce credible projections or perfect their pitch. These rushed assets make it impossible to convince investors that they are an investable entrepreneur. Remember, a typical funding round takes three to six months to close and preparing the critical fundraising assets will take you a number of weeks before that even starts.

Don't wait until you've burned through your current funds before you consider seeking investment. Start the process now. Even if you don't have all the key fundraising assets in place there's nothing stopping you beginning the process of building a network of investors.

When you begin seeking investment too late you become desperate. It shows in your approach, your body language and your pitch. Investors don't invest in the needy. If they did, they'd call themselves philanthropists. You don't want to come across as a charity case, you want to be seen as an investable entrepreneur. Don't leave your pursuit of investment until you *need* the money. Remember, seeking investment is a strategic activity to leverage capital to implement your growth strategy – not a stopgap when cashflow fails.

My advice is to act now. Start working on becoming an investable entrepreneur as soon as you finish reading this book. The best place to start is completing the Robot Mascot PitchReady scorecard at www. pitchready.co.uk to discover the areas in which you perform well and the areas which you need to spend time developing.

Mistake Two: I'm in this on my own

For some reason, founders believe that they need to be able to do everything themselves. They need to struggle with the finances, spend days writing and rewriting their business plan, draft their own legal documentation and spend sleepless nights agonising over how to articulate their message.

The truth is that most successful entrepreneurs surround themselves with experts who are better than they are. Founders have this strange notion that, if they haven't created the business plan, financial projections or pitch materials themselves, then they've failed at being an entrepreneur. This just isn't the case. Think of it this way: do you think the CEOs of multi-national corporations spend hundreds of thousands of pounds using the likes of PwC or KPMG to create a business plan because they're unable to do it themselves? Of course not; they bring in firms with a good reputation because it adds credibility to their cause and reduces the likelihood that investors will question their assumptions.

Investors can immediately tell when assets have been created by the founder. These lack focus, are over-ambitious and miss important details. With high-quality, independently produced assets you can increase your chances of success and access investment on much better terms than you otherwise would.

When working with an expert team (whether advisors, consultants or an agency), you have to be prepared to dedicate time to providing them with the information they need. They'll then add their own objective perspective and do additional research to help support your claims. Some will achieve this through extensive interviews and multiple workshops with you. At Robot Mascot, we've found that by replacing this process with our online platform, PitchPrep, we're able to make the whole process more efficient and more streamlined for all involved. However you choose to approach it, it's important to remember that behind every investable entrepreneur there is a highly performing team.

Mistake Three: Lose sight of the big picture

Raising investment isn't a quick process; you'll most likely spend at least half a year from start to finish. During this time, it's easy to be drawn back into the day-to-day operations of your business. When this happens, you get tunnel vision. You lose sight of the wider strategic vision and miss critical factors that make the difference between success and failure.

By drawing yourself away from the day-today operations of the business to consider the big picture you'll completely transform your business. I've had many clients comment to me how incredibly inspiring going through the preparation phase of 'The Six Principles of the Perfect Pitch' was for them. By spending time away from the operations of the business and using this time to think strategically about their business through our PitchPrep tool, they were suddenly able to see things about their business they'd never noticed before. In some cases, they massively improved their business model, in others they created improved product offerings that delivered much greater value for their customers. Others simply felt inspired as they reflected on what they'd created so far and planned the details of their future path.

Embodying the investable entrepreneur

We've spoken a lot in this book about having the assets in place to show that you're an investable entrepreneur. But there's one thing I cannot help you with, and that is your own mindset. I can tell you what you need to do, and I can help you create the pitch materials you'll need to convince investors, but I can't give you the confidence to believe you're worthy of their money.

I can, however, tell you what common traits I see in successful and investable entrepreneurs. For me, and I'm sure many investors, it's obvious from the moment you speak with a founder for the first time whether or not they have what it takes to succeed.

Trait One: Confidence

Some founders are terrified by the prospect of raising investment. Sometimes that's because they're scared of pitching in public, worried about the scrutiny they'll be putting themselves under or because they feel they're going around begging for money.

I find that, once my clients have all the critical fundraising assets in place, their demeanour changes. By going through the process of thinking strategically about their business and developing this into inspiring communication, they themselves become more inspired. This has a knock-on effect on their performance in the boardroom. They no longer have impostor syndrome. They believe in themselves; they believe in their business; and they realise they're offering a great opportunity that an investor would be lucky to be a part of.

As you begin pitching, you'll realise you have a business that people want to know more about. You'll win more fans than you will critics and you'll soon realise that you're not begging for cash; you are offering investors an opportunity to make large sums of money.

Trait Two: Relentlessness

At times it will feel like a long road ahead. Before you get into the fundraising groove, you're likely to spend some time stumbling around in the dark. It may feel you're not getting anywhere. But trust me, you are. You're learning on the job, as you have done throughout your time as an entrepreneur.

No one starts their first business with experience of starting a business, yet you have started and are growing a successful enterprise. You've learned loads along the way, and second time around you'll get to where you're heading a million times quicker. It's no different with fundraising.

If you've never undertaken a fundraising campaign before then you'll definitely make some mistakes.

Investable entrepreneurs, however, learn from those mistakes and adapt their thinking and processes quickly. This is a great quality that every investor is looking for.

Trait Three: Conviction

You should expect plenty of knock-backs. Even with the perfect pitch, perfect projections and perfect plan, investors may tell you your idea stands no chance. Don't listen to them. Have conviction in your ability, know that if setbacks present themselves, you'll be able to adapt and come out the other side stronger.

Think of all the times you've done exactly that to get to this point (perhaps even mention these to the investor that doubts you). You know your business and your market better than anyone else. Don't fundamentally change what you're doing because an investor who's known you for five minutes says you should. Believe in yourself, believe in your plan and believe in your idea.

When an investable entrepreneur gets knocked down, they get back up again. Every step backwards gives them the opportunity to adjust their approach and take three steps forwards. You have to be willing to put yourself out there and take the rough with the smooth. The more investors you meet, the better your chance of finding investors that align with your vision.

Case study: The original investable entrepreneur

To end this book, I want to share a story that encapsulates everything outlined in the last 14 chapters; a story that epitomises what it means to be an investable entrepreneur.

I met Tony Pauley in 2018 after an introduction from an associate. I was immediately blown away by his story; the story I'm going to share with you now. It shows that if you apply 'The Six Principles of the Perfect Pitch', develop your critical fundraising assets and implement a strategic fundraising campaign then you really can achieve incredible investment success.

Tony was on the founding team that achieved the most successful early-stage fundraising campaign by a UK company, ever. The business was in the financial sector, and back in 2008 they started pitching their idea to investors. The product was called a partnership mortgage. It was the first shared-home-ownership scheme in the UK and was similar to what we now know as Help to Buy – although they were selling the product to a different kind of consumer. Tony fondly recalls his fundraising success:

> 'It's the most ever raised by a UK startup. We raised £65 million in seed funding. As far as I am aware, we still hold the record for the largest ever seed round.'

They were the original investable entrepreneurs. Unknown to them they had implemented 'The Six Principles of the Perfect Pitch' and demonstrated the key traits of an investable entrepreneur. Tony's story goes to show the incredible things that can be achieved when you implement the methodologies in this book.

The secret to Tony's success

Tony puts the secret to his success down to two things: credibility and resilience. The first thing Tony and his team ensured was that the business plan and financial projections were both very appealing and completely rock-solid. Nothing was left to chance. When raising £65 million, having unimpeachable foundations to their pitch would be absolutely essential. Through a lot of hard work, they were able to demonstrate quite clearly that in almost any market situation they would make money, as Tony explains.

'If the property market went up – we would make money. If the property market went down – we would make money. No matter what happened, we would make money.'

Tony had executed the preparation phase of 'The Six Principles of the Perfect Pitch' to perfection. When his team went to pitch their business to investors, they were able to present a viable plan for commercial success alongside credible financial projections. They'd put the effort in, they'd done their research and they'd thought of all possible outcomes. This would later prove to be vital in bringing the deal off.

Secondly, Tony embodied the core traits of an investable entrepreneur: confidence, conviction and relentlessness. With such eye-watering numbers at stake they had priced themselves out of the conventional seed investment routes. But they were not phased, they had confidence in their plan and their fundraising goals. Instead, the team approached private equity firms, more suited to later-stage investments. This led to lots and lots of rejections, as Tony recalls:

'It took the better part of three years talking to private equity investors before somebody was willing to take a really deep look at the plan and the projections. But eventually it worked. We got the investment only because the business model was so incredibly robust.'

Tony could have easily given up after six to nine months, but the team kept going and going until they got the *yes* that changed their lives for good. But not in the way you would expect.

You can never have enough money

With £65 million in the bank you would have thought that Tony was onto an instant success. Rarely is the life of an entrepreneur that simple. Even with £65 million to play with, building a startup is a roller coaster.

The plan was to achieve Financial Conduct Authority authorisation within six months. They had all of the things in place that would mean that should have been easily achievable – they had the capital, the product and the team. However, when it came to it, their proposal terrified the regulator. Tony puts this down to their having a product the regulators didn't understand, a lot of money, and a powerful board of directors (which included some of the UK's top CEOs, CFOs and even an ex-Cabinet Minister).

Instead of taking six months, it took two-and-a-half years to get authorised. In the meantime, they were paying the whole team as they needed the staff on the books in order to get authorisation. Eventually, they were left with no choice but to take the government to court over the issue, costing them £20 million in legal fees.

By the time they did achieve regulation the business was almost bankrupt. They'd run out of cash before doing any business: £65 million had been spent while they waited for FCA authorisation. Tony recalls:

> 'It was one of those things; the investment should have been plenty. But life kicks you in the teeth. We came very, very close to running out of money – we were six weeks from being dead.'

Eventually they got back on their feet. They hired the head of sales from Nationwide who came in and pivoted the product towards buy-to-let landlords. It was at this point that the product started to fly off the shelf and now the business is doing extremely well.

Lessons learned

Tony has learned a number of valuable lessons from the highs and lows of raising the UK's largest seed investment, but his best advice is to nail the communication:

> 'When I look back at our pitch, on every single page we had the acronym 'NIM': it means Net Interest Margin. The reason for this was that we were seeking investment from people who ran banks. In banks, all they think about is Net Interest Margin.

> 'You've got to use the language of the people you're trying to get to invest in you. For example, we couldn't possibly talk about 'software as a service' metrics to banks, as they just don't care – they don't understand them.

> 'If you know who your investors are and what language they use, then your job becomes much easier. There's more money in the market than there are good ideas. They're just looking for a credible place to put it.'

And with that, Tony had hit on the fundamental theme of this book; the underlying premise explained back in Chapter 1. To successfully raise investment, you must speak the language of an investor. You must address their concerns, justify the risk and pitch to them on their terms. You must prepare a plan that demonstrates commercial viability, projections that justify the risks and a pitch that inspires them to follow you on your vision. When you can do that, you can achieve incredible things, just like Tony Pauley did.

Summary

You now know the three mistakes you must avoid if you're to become an investable entrepreneur, as well as the three traits you'll need to embrace to be a success. You realise that there will be many twists, turns and knock-backs along the way, but having carefully considered all of the critical fundraising assets, and having produced a perfect pitch, you know (and believe) that you will raise investment. You've seen for yourself what can be achieved when you implement the ideas in this book. There really is no limit to your success.

Summary

Entrepreneurs have great ideas. They have the ability to make them a success. But the odds tell me that they'll most likely fail to raise the investment they need to make their dreams a reality. Despite all the effort, despite the hype and despite their willingness to succeed, they'll fail.

The reason for this isn't down to their ideas. It isn't down to their ability to grow a successful business. And it isn't down to their lack of ambition. It's simply down to their ability to communicate with investors.

Only if you're able to show that you're highly resourceful, understand the financial risks and rewards and have a plan for commercial success; if you're able to inspire investors to join you in

207

achieving your vision; only then will you hear those magic words, 'Yes, I'd like to invest in your business'.

Imagine what that feels like for a second. After all the hard work bootstrapping your business, after the emotional pain, the hard graft and the sleepless nights, hearing that 'Yes, I want to invest' will be the most satisfying feeling in the world. When you get that first 'Yes' it will be hard to remain professional and composed. Inside you'll be wanting to scream, do a dance and give the investor a great big hug.

Imagine then, the feeling that follows when you hear five *yeses* and have enough committed to close your round: the nervousness as you send out the legal paperwork, and the elation when you look in your bank account to see more zeros than you've ever seen on a bank statement in your life. Because of the sacrifice, because of the effort, because of the dream it enables, that will feel a million times more satisfying than the luck of winning the lottery. The two cannot compare.

This is what life feels like as an investable entrepreneur. No matter how many times you raise investment, the highs that come from success do not fade. I've seen experienced entrepreneurs act like kids in a candy store when they get the news that they've closed an investment round. I watch as they struggle to contain their excitement.

When you have the formulae for becoming an investable entrepreneur, when you have the methodology for creating the perfect pitch, this feeling, this success, becomes so easily repeated. Time and again you can raise investment, close deals and build brilliant businesses.

You now have these secrets. Use what I've shared in this book wisely. Master the craft of communicating with investors, embrace the transition into an investable entrepreneur and you will succeed. You'll defy the odds and be in an elite group of your peers. You'll be in the top 1% who successfully raise investment.

What's Next

Take the scorecard

Discover your PitchReady score and assess your current ability to raise investment. In less than five minutes you'll discover whether you're in a position to capture an investor's interest and aise investment. You'll receive a tailored report with tips on how to improve your score and work towards becoming an investable entrepreneur. Simply visit www.pitchready. co.uk.

Review this book

If you enjoyed this book, then please take the time to review it on Amazon. Send a screen shot of your review, or a link to a blog post that features this book, and you'll be sent a complementary ticket to one of my Fundraising Strategy Sessions.

Join the community

Join my Facebook group 'Investable Entrepreneur' to engage with like-minded entrepreneurs, keep up to date with the latest investment trends and receive ongoing support and advice from me. I post regular content and share current best practices for convincing investors your business is the one to back. You can join the group here: www.facebook.com/groups/investable.entrepreneur.

If you don't do Facebook, then you can connect with me on LinkedIn where I share similar insights: www.linkedin.com/in/jamescchurch/.

Discover more about being a successful entrepreneur

The Robot Mascot blog contains many articles written by the team at Robot Mascot and our strategic partners on the subjects of raising investment, building a brand and scaling your business. It's a hub of information to give you the support and guidance you need to build a successful business. Simply log on to www.robotmascot.co.uk/articles.

Access free resources

Robot Mascot have produced a number of free resources to support you in creating the perfect pitch, plan and projections. You can access the free resources at www.robotmascot.co.uk/free-resources.

Book me as a speaker

If you run a group, accelerator, incubator or event that is focused on founders and entrepreneurs then perhaps you'd like me to talk about raising investment. I can cover any of the themes in this book, and more besides. Visit www.robotmascot.co.uk/james-church to book me for your meeting or event.

References

Audretsch, David B (2012) 'Determinants of High-Growth Entrepreneurship: Report prepared for the OECD/DBA International Workshop on High-growth firms: local policies and local determinants', www.oecd.org/cfe/leed/Audretsch_determinants%20of%20high-growth%20firms.pdf, accessed 5 August 2020

Collister, Patrick (2017) *How To Use Innovation and Creativity in the Workplace* (Bluebird)

Eisenberg, Harris (2018) 'Humans process visual data better', Thermopylae Sciences and Technology, www.t-sciences.com/news/humans-process-visual-data-better, accessed 5 August 2020

Espinal, Carlos and Cobb, Matthew (2015) *Fundraising Field Guide* (Reedsy)

Horne, David B (2019) *Add Then Multiply* (Rethink Press)

Jonikas, Dr Donatas (2017) *Startup Evolution Curve* (CreateSpace)

Jobber, David and Ellis-Chadwick, Fiona (2013) *Principle and Practice of Marketing* (McGraw-Hill)

Landa, Robin (2013) *Graphic Design Solutions* (Wadsworth Publishing)

Priestley, Daniel (2017) *24 Assets* (Rethink Press)

Priestley, Daniel (2014) *Key Person of Influence* (Rethink Press)

Sandler, David H and Mattson, David (2015) *You Can't Teach a Kid to Ride a Bike at a Seminar* (McGraw-Hill)

Wainman, Ted (2015) *How To Talk Finance* (Pearson)

Watt, James (2015) *Business for Punks: Break All the Rules – the BrewDog Way* (Penguin)

Acknowledgements

The first person to thank is my wife, Rachael. We met when I was 18, just a few weeks before heading off to university, and have been through this whole journey together. Since that first date you've been nothing but supportive of my career, allowing me the freedom to follow my dreams and passions. Together we've celebrated many successes (in life and in business), but you've also been there through the failures, sticking by me, believing in me and willing me to succeed. Without your love and support I wouldn't be the man I am today.

To Nicolas Ruston, my business partner. You're my mentor, business partner and best friend. As the creative director at the branding agency that gave me my first job, you took me under your wing and taught me everything I know about design and creativity. Your mentorship and friendship have not only made me a better creative, but also a better version of me. We've shared many highs and lows over the years: working as a creative team at various branding agencies, our first experience in business with our agency Craft/Associates, our first business failure with that same agency and the incredible journey we've shared building Robot Mascot to what it is today. I'll forever be grateful to you for suggesting I join you as co-founder of Robot Mascot, I've never looked back.

To my mum and dad who have always been there and have always supported me to achieve my goals. Thank you for giving me the life skills, attitude and guidance that have fostered creativity, entrepreneurship and a driven determination to succeed.

Thinking more specifically about the writing of this book, I have to start with Daniel Priestley, co-founder and CEO of Dent Global. For believing in the Robot Mascot vision, for your guidance and wisdom and for your continued support, I'm truly grateful. Completing the *Key Person of Influence* and *24 Asset* accelerators has been life-changing – this is only the start of our journey; I cannot wait to see where it ends.

To Professor John French, who believed in us from the start: you offered us crucial advice and mentorship and first set us on a journey to explore opportunities in the tech sector; without your insight who knows where we'd be today.

To all the investors that I interviewed for this book, in particular James Merryweather, Jason Warren, Laura Harnett, Jerneja Loncar, Ranvir Saggu and Sacha Waters for giving me so much of your incredibly precious time. Also, to all those investors over the years (of whom there are too many to list) who have shared coffee with me, generously giving insights that have allowed me to positively impact the success of hundreds of founders – you all know who you are.

To Robot Mascot's amazing clients who have agreed to be featured in this book so other entrepreneurs can learn from their successes; Benjamin Carew, Wesley Payne, Zoë Desmond, Abiodun Elohim, Andries Smit, Conor Svensson, Esteban Lupin, Mohammad Uz-Zaman and Lionel Bernard: your support means so much, thank you.

To all of the extended Robot Mascot family – our network of partners and associates that are there to call upon when we need advice and are there to help and support our incredible clients: Ermine Amies, Leslie Azam, John Burroughs, Neil Garner, David B Horne, Jonathan Keeling, James McKerracher, Andrew Moon, Avril Mulcahy, Cornelius Reithdorf, David Reynolds, Matthew Roberts, Anthony Rose, Richard Ross, Hannah Smith, Kevin Smith, Tom Sutton and too many others for me to list here. Your support over the years has been invaluable. You have my deepest thanks.

To Tony Pauley for sharing his incredible story with me and allowing me to include it as a case study in this book.

To my beta readers, Joe Brouder, John Davies, David B Horne, James McKerracher, James Merryweather and Conor Svensson, thank you for your time and commitment to this project. Your feedback, insights and scrutiny ensured this book went to press at its best.

Finally, to all the founders I've worked with over the years, you've made this the best job in the world. Being able to watch from behind the scenes as you successfully raise the investment you need to live your business dreams is what keeps me doing what I'm doing.

The Author

As the chief operating officer and co-founder of Robot Mascot, James runs the UK's leading pitch specialist. He's helped hundreds of founders and entrepreneurs understand how to create a winning pitch and assisted them to perfectly position their investment opportunity so that they can better convince investors.

Having come from a branding and marketing background, James has always believed that when great innovation meets inspiring communication incredible things can happen. It has the power to change the world, inspire a movement and build brilliant brands.

James has always had a great skill in applying creative principles to achieve commercial outcomes. His ability to see beyond the principles of design and communication and understand the nuances of business strategy has helped create the unique investor communication services offered by Robot Mascot.

After conducting intensive research with hundreds of investors and entrepreneurs over a three-year period, James created 'The Six Principles of the Perfect Pitch'. The success of this methodology led to Robot Mascot developing partnerships with some of the leading players in the tech and investment sectors and they soon developed a reputation as the UK's leading pitch agency.

James has been featured in *Entrepreneur* magazine, on numerous industry blogs and podcasts, runs mentoring sessions at Tech Hub, Google Campus and Runway East, and has delivered mastermind sessions for SeedLegals, The Chartered Institute of Marketing and the University of East Anglia.

If you would like to connect with James, or send him a direct message, you can reach out via LinkedIn at www.linkedin.com/in/jamescchurch.